An Irish Word a Day

Hector Ó hEochagáin is a TV and radio presenter. He co-hosted Ireland's most popular podcast with Tommy Tiernan and Laurita Blewitt. He has spent the past 23 years travelling to some of the most incredible places on earth for his long-running and much-loved popular travel show on TG4. At the forefront of the Irish-language revival, his previous book – *The Irish Words You Should Know* – won best Irish-Published Book of the Year at the An Post Irish Book Awards. He lives in County Galway.

An Irish Word a Day*

HECTOR Ó hEOCHAGÁIN

*365 ways to speak Irish every day

GILL BOOKS

Gill Books
Hume Avenue
Park West
Dublin 12
www.gillbooks.ie

Gill Books is an imprint of M.H. Gill and Co.

© Hector Ó hEochagáin 2025

9781804583449

Original design by Bartek Janczak
Typeset by Padraig McCormack
Edited by Catherine Gough
Illustrations by Stephen Synnott
Copy edited by Anna Kealy
Proofread by Paula Elmore and Fidelma Ní Ghallchobhair
Printed and bound in Great Britain by Clays Ltd, Elcograf S.p.A.
This book is typeset in Pro 11.5pt on 14pt, FreightText.

The paper used in this book comes from the wood pulp of sustainably managed forests.

All rights reserved.
No part of this publication may be copied, reproduced or transmitted in any form or by any means, without written permission of the publishers.

To the best of our knowledge, this book complies in full with the requirements of the General Product Safety Regulation (GPSR). For further information and help with any safety queries, please contact us at *productsafety@gill.ie*.

A CIP catalogue record for this book is available from the British Library.

5 4 3

*Do mo bhean chéile Dympna agus mo leaids
Rían agus Shane. Grá mór i gcónaí, x.*

Introduction

To be sitting here writing the introduction to my second book about Irish is surreal. It's mad to think that I'm about to share more brilliant and enriching Irish words and phrases with you, and I'm so very proud that this language adventure continues. The reaction to and love for *The Irish Words You Should Know* has been incredible. It was amazing to hear the words that caught people's attention, like *gafa* (busy), *scaití* (sometimes) and *ar bís* (buzzing), but nothing could compare to the love you all had for *loinnir*. Someone got in touch to tell me they had christened their new boat in the Claddagh *Loinnir*, and I was sent photos of the word being tattooed on readers' skin. *Dochreidte*! (Unreal!)

I think *loinnir* caught on because it does that thing the Irish language does so beautifully. It's a word straight from nature – the glistening of the sun on the waves – that has been recycled to mean something social: the merry feeling you get after early pints. I have more words like that for you in this book, ones like *fonn* (p. 299), which means to be in the mood for something (*fonn ort*), but also to be able to pick up and play a tune (*an bhfuil fonn agat?*) – because the Irish language knows that our moods are the tunes of our bodies, and we dance to their rhythm. Every word in every language is formed and forged from the landscape, and it's in this landscape that it lives and breathes. Irish is a river that's always flowing, and we just have to dip our toes in. We can hear its *sruth* (current, p. 67) if we listen out for it: on the radio, in schools, in cafés and even in our own minds – if we open ourselves up to it.

Irish has blessed us with so many ways to say things. Each word is used exactly when it's needed, spoken when the situation calls for it. So now I come to you with a word for every day of the year. I harvested them from anywhere and everywhere: words that popped into my head, words that I plucked from conversations, words I heard on TG4 or on Raidió na Gaeltachta and words that came to me from the landscape. At the beginning of the project, I bought a small, ornate notebook in a shop *fionnuar* (cool, p. 206) in Clifden and took it with me to Australia and New Zealand, where I was filming for the TG4 travel show in early 2025. I found myself scribbling words like *ollmhór* (gigantic, p. 190) and *gráinnín gainimh* (grain of sand, p. 189) as we drove through some of the most remote places on the planet. Even in the outback of Australia, Irish was there waiting for me.

Now all these words have come together to fill the pages of this book, and I hope the stories I've written to describe them fill up your *samhlaíocht* (imagination, p. 80) and help you feel their vibe. I want you to learn these words, to share them, engage with them and try to use them. That's really the key here. There will be words that are new to you and, if you went to school in Ireland, words you already know but probably forgot about. Our language is rich and we can enjoy using the everyday words as much as we enjoy learning a fancy new one; *tearmann* (sanctuary, p. 22) is no better or worse than *bronntanas* (present, p. 325). We should give ourselves credit for the amount of Irish words we already know from school. There's just something inside that stops us, an embarrassment that we can't string sentences together. But this language is yours to use, no matter how much or little of it you know. Throwing a word or phrase *as Gaeilge* into your English-language conversations and texts is how we revive a language – one word at a time and one day at a time. We dole out the Spanish 'siesta' no problem when we want a little afternoon nap, so why not use *sos beag* (small break, p. 332) instead?

I'm excited to find out which words from this book take flight, the words you name your boat after or get tattooed on your arm. So once again I say *go raibh míle* to this language of ours. It's ready to greet you when you want to call in; all you have to do is walk up to the door and knock. *Beidh fáilte romhat i gcónaí!* (You will always be welcome!)

1 EANÁIR / 1 JANUARY

Oidhreacht
Heritage

[eye-rocht]

Tá an oidhreacht is saibhre ar domhan againn sa tír seo.
We have the richest heritage in the world in this country.

There has been an awakening in Ireland about our heritage. I see it all the time when random people stop me to talk. One fella walked up to me and took his phone out to show me a photo of some standing stones on the top of a hill, and he says to me, 'I bet you don't know where that is.' But I did. It was the standing stones at Loughcrew near Oldcastle in County Meath. It's a magical hill full of passage tombs that's known as 'The Hill of the Witch'. It was this man's favourite place in the world. He's not the first person, nor will he be the last, to stop me while I'm shopping or getting petrol to talk about our *oidhreacht*.

I think about our *oidhreacht* every time I pass a massive boulder in a village in Claregalway. I've been driving past it for about 20 years. And then I see this guy on *The Tommy Tiernan Show* who lifts stones for a living. His name is David Keohan, but he's better known as Indiana Stones. Lifting big stones has been done in Ireland for hundreds of years as a show of strength. Back in the day, warriors would lift these stones high enough so that the wind would blow underneath them, then they'd put them back down where they found them and that was that. I was fascinated. I thought this was the best thing I'd ever heard. Indiana Stones had been all over the country heaving stones, and then one Saturday as I'm driving by the Claregalway boulder, I see him standing there with a bunch of lads. The massive stone I had seen propped up against the wall of a house was about to be lifted in a tradition that stretched back centuries. That's what *oidhreacht* is all about.

2 EANÁIR / 2 JANUARY

Bolg
Tummy/belly

[bull-ug]

Tá sé in am fáil réidh le bolg na Nollag.
It's time to get rid of this Christmas belly.

Doesn't *bolg* sound like it should look? Big and round and soft and lovely. An Irish belly is a work of art, sculpted by time like the Cliffs of Moher. It provides coverage and protection; there's no harm to it. We should celebrate our *bolgs* like we celebrate a big baby.

I have many tattoos honouring our Irish folklore that all mean something to me – my two arms now bear Celtic symbols. But the first tattoo I ever got was a small Fear Bolg. In Irish mythology, the Fir Bolg were the fourth group of people said to have settled in Ireland. I wanted a symbol of ancient Ireland as my first tattoo, so I got a little guy with a lovely *bolg* standing proud with a long spear. I got the bus up from Navan to Dublin to get it done in The Mint off Moore Street. It was one of the busiest tattoo places in Dublin in the 1980s and '90s. Apparently the *bolg* in 'Fir Bolg' means 'bags', but to me the Fir Bolg were the original Men of the Belly, and all the *bolgs* putting pressure on shirt buttons across the country are their descendants.

3 EANÁIR / 3 JANUARY

Spideog
Robin

[spid-owg]

D'fhéach mé amach an fhuinneog agus bhí spideog bhroinndearg ann.
I looked out the window and there was a robin redbreast.

4 EANÁIR / 4 JANUARY

Spéis
Interest

[spaysh]

Tá spéis agam sa cheol.
I'm interested in music.

This is a word for all levels of interest – you could be interested in football or politics or knitting or stamps, or just interested in hearing more of a friend's story. Spéis is a great thing to have.

5 EANÁIR / 5 JANUARY

Lardrús
Larder

[laurd-roos]

Bhí an lardrús lán go béal le bia.
The larder was full to the brim with food.

Larders are back in vogue with the hundred-grand kitchens on *Room to Improve*, but my godparents had the larder of all larders back in the day.

We would drive to their house near Moate for a visit when we were kids, and we loved it. The sound of driving over the cattle grid in our Cortina told us we had arrived. The road wound on for another half a mile and then we'd see it as we rounded the last bend: a big country house with a massive garden. They even had a swimming pool – and this was 1970s Ireland. And it was Westmeath. Unfortunately, there was no swimming to be done, because it never had any water in it, but we would still kick a ball around it or use it as a tennis court.

My favourite thing about visiting them was the larder. The kitchen was always warm and welcoming and the larder was always cool and full of food. I knew there would be a tin of biscuits in there for us.

That larder was in its natural environment. My godparents were farming people. There were stuffed foxes and pheasants in display cases, the carpeted stairs creaked, and every hour the grandfather clock shouted 'BING BONG!' at us. Going to the toilet at night was a bit spooky, but to me as a child this house was like Narnia. It was enchanting.

I knew when we went to visit there would always be a welcome hug and food from the larder for us. Larders in modern houses just don't fit. They're glorified presses.

6 EANÁIR / 6 JANUARY

Scuaine
Queue

[skoo-nya]

Sháraigh an leaid seo an scuaine san aerphort.
This lad jumped the queue in the airport.

I can practically hear teachers in national schoolyards shouting, 'Scuaine' or 'Ina líne'. But asking a load of children to get in a queue is an invitation for messing, and it doesn't change as you get older. Irish people think of a scuaine *as a time to have the craic.*

7 EANÁIR / 7 JANUARY

Gallúnach
Soap

[gall-oo-nock]

Chuimil sí an gallúnach idir a lámha.
She rubbed the soap between her hands.

The first place I lived in Dublin, as a 17-year-old student, was a bedsit in Cabra Park. It was a three-storey house in Phibsboro that was in the shadow of a big church during the day and lit up by the floodlights of Dalymount Park at night. It epitomised the accommodation of country people who came up to Dublin to study or work. It was horrific. There was a wardrobe, a one-cylinder stove, a sink so small you wouldn't even find it in a camper van, and a pull-out bed that I shared with my brother Freddie. And there was no toilet – that was on the second floor and shared with the other residents.

The main feature of the communal toilet was a bar of Imperial Leather soap that was stuck to the sink. It looked like it had been there since the 1970s. If this bar of soap had been on the set of a movie, it would have been genius. Imperial Leather was supposed to be a luxury brand and here it was, with a single hair wrapped around it, stuck to a sink in Phibsboro.

Rosco, the cameraman on our TG4 travel show, is a soap aficionado. He's well past the Palmolive. The first thing he does when we're away, whether it's Kingston, Bangkok or New York City, is go to a local shop to buy the local soap. I know that within five minutes of arriving at a nice hotel, he'll text me to ask if I'm using the fancy little soaps in my room. And I have no problem handing them over, because to me *gallúnach* will always be a bar of Imperial Leather stuck to a sink in a bedsit.

8 EANÁIR / 8 JANUARY

Rún a dhéanamh
Resolution

[roon a yayn-iv]

Rinne mé rún le haghaidh na bliana nua dul go dtí an gym.
I made a resolution to go to the gym in the New Year.

It's a week into the New Year and you've already given up your resolution. You spent €400 on a gym membership and you've been twice. You haven't done a squat in over six months, so you're so sore you can't even bend down to put on your boxer shorts or knickers. You're walking down the stairs like a flamingo, and it takes you seven minutes to go down ten steps. You get to the car, but you can't get in without gripping the roof and sort of swinging yourself in. You eventually fall into the driver's seat and think to yourself, 'What have I done?'

January is lactic acid month, and the gyms make a killing. If it's not the gym, it's another company trying to sell you something. I don't buy into resolutions. The closest I ever got to making one was writing an affirmation on a piece of paper and putting it in the pocket of a shirt in my wardrobe to keep it safe. The problem was, six months later, I couldn't find the piece of paper, so I couldn't remember what I was trying to manifest.

The word 'resolution' doesn't really have a place in the Irish language. It was imported from English, which is why it sounds awkward: *rinne mé rún* sort of translates as 'have an intention to'. Our Irish-speaking ancestors didn't have a word for 'resolution' because they knew they are a load of rubbish. Instead of focusing on the beginning of January, we should be opening our minds to the simple things every day. If you see the beautiful in the ordinary, it'll be better for your health than any overpriced and underused gym membership – and you won't have any trouble putting your boxers on.

9 EANÁIR / 9 JANUARY

Amaideach
Ridiculous

[am-a-dyuch]

Ná bí amaideach.
Don't be ridiculous.

Amaideach *is related to the word* amadán, *meaning* 'eejit'. *It's for those moments when a friend says, 'Will we go to the Europa League Final?' a day before the match.* 'Ná bí amaideach!' (*Don't be ridiculous!*)

10 EANÁIR / 10 JANUARY

Plúiríní sneachta
Snowdrops

[ploor-een-ee shnokh-ta]

Tá na plúiríní sneachta amuigh ag bun an bhalla.
The snowdrops are out at the bottom of the wall.

This translates as 'little bits of snow', which makes me think of dust molecules. It feels miniature. It's the first growth of the year in January when you see the tiny little heads of plúiríní sneachta *peeking above the ground. After all the darkness, rain and storms of the winter, life is on the way again.*

11 EANÁIR / 11 JANUARY

Ispín faoi fhuidreamh
Battered sausage

[ish-peen fwee yewdrav]

Fuair me sceallóga móra agus dhá ispíní faoi fhuidreamh tigh Ezio aréir san Uaimh.
I got a large chips and two battered sausages in Ezio's last night in Navan.

12 EANÁIR / 12 JANUARY

Dinglisí
Tickles

[ding-lish-ee]

An bhfuil aon dinglisí agat?
Do you have any tickles?

Tickles spark a happy memory for me. They've always played an important part in our house. Every day, when my boys would come home from school, we'd play a tickle game. I'd tickle them, and then the challenge was they would have to tickle me so much that I'd fall off the sofa. They were about eight or nine and it was the heyday of WWE. The boys had all the little figurines – John Cena, the Undertaker – they were mad into it. So we'd have our own WWE smackdowns at home, but with tickles.

I still tickle them now, even though they're 19 and 21. They're almost as strong as me, but I know if I get them under the chin they'll be gone. There's a lovely thing about not forgetting how much fun we had with tickles when they were kids.

I think it's important to know the *dinglisí* weak spots for everyone in your household. Now, I don't mean sneaking up behind someone when they're doing the dishes or grabbing their bare feet and tickling them – that's not fun. I mean the proper tickle zones of your kids or your parents or your partner. It's a secret weapon.

13 EANÁIR / 13 JANUARY

Tearmann
Sanctuary

[char-min]

Is é an gairdín cúil mo thearmann.
My back garden is my sanctuary.

The first time I heard the word *tearmann* I was working for Coláiste na bhFiann, an Irish-language organisation that bought out an old hospital in the village of Coole in Westmeath near Lough Derravaragh. I knew about Lough Derravaragh from the *Children of Lir*, but I'd never seen it, even though it's just outside Mullingar. The whole area is steeped in *oidhreacht* (heritage, p. 11), so Coláiste na bhFiann decided to call this old building Tearmann Lir – the Sanctuary of Lir.

Tearmann is the closest word in Irish to describe what a temple is. It makes me think of going to Thailand and seeing a Buddhist temple. It's a word for stillness and peace.

However, right beside Tearmann Lir on the shores of Lough Derravaragh, we were running military-style camps. I was doing drills with 14- and 15-year-old lads all dressed in camouflage gear and speaking Irish. It was called Campa Fiannais. Every morning we would have a flag ceremony, fish in the lake, cook outdoors, and then spend the afternoon in the local wood doing manoeuvres. We'd paint our faces with black stuff, lie on the ground and shoot toy guns at each other – it was like paintball without the paint.

In retrospect, Tearmann Lir wasn't all that peaceful, but it was a kind of Irish-speaking sanctuary for the teenage lads. Now my *tearmann* is my back garden. It's wherever you can switch off and find peace – your local park, the beach, up a mountain. It doesn't even have to be a place; you can have an inner *tearmann*. It's a beautiful word that makes me feel calm just saying it.

14 EANÁIR / 14 JANUARY

Cíoch
Breast

[kee-och]

Bhí an leanbh ina codladh ar chíocha a máthar.
The baby was sleeping on her mother's breasts.

In Irish there's one beautiful way to say 'breast', and it's a far more comforting word than the 10 different ways we have to say it in English. Cíoch is a place to comfort a child; it's a place of peace and warmth; it's where life is nurtured.

15 EANÁIR / 15 JANUARY

Sciodar
Slurry

[shcyudd-er]

Bhí boladh sciodair ag teacht isteach tríd an bhfuinneog.
The smell of slurry was coming in the window.

I used to have a slot on my breakfast show on 2FM called 'Medium-Sized Town, Fairly Big Story'. My friend Ronan Casey would come in and read out an interesting bit of news from towns all over the country, but I'll never forget when we came across the story of a young guy from Carrickmacross who was refused entrance to a nightclub.

Most people would just go home disappointed, but this lad came back an hour later with his dad's slurry tank, pulled up to the entrance and fired about a ton of slurry all over the nightclub. It was such a spectacle that it made the nine o'clock news.

Now, you either know the smell of slurry or you don't. I live in a country area, and when they're spreading slurry, the smell is everywhere – it makes its way through your triple-glazing and gets into your clothes. Can you imagine the smell of that nightclub? The stink of *sciodar* off the main door, the cloakroom, the bouncers ... But this young lad was standing up for his rights, and you can't deny that the slurry dump was a magnificent form of protest.

16 EANÁIR / 16 JANUARY

Druid
Starling

[drid]

Chonaic mé na mílte druideanna sa spéir aréir.
I saw thousands of starlings in the sky last night.

———————————

In 2021 James Crombie's breathtaking photo of a murmuration of starlings won Irish Photo of the Year. Mother Nature gives us these things to open up our eyes to and behold.

17 EANÁIR / 17 JANUARY

Stail
Stallion

[stall]

Ceann de na staileanna ba cháiliúla in Éirinn ab ea Galileo.
One of the most famous stallions in Ireland was Galileo.

———————————

When champion horses retire from track and racing, some of them become the kings of reproduction. All these great staileanna *do is eat, sleep and make foals.*

18 EANÁIR / 18 JANUARY

Láir
Mare

[lawr]

Is í Honeysuckle ceann de na láracha is fearr in Éirinn.
Honeysuckle is one of the best mares in Ireland.

I love horse racing. It's one of my passions. In Ireland we have thousands of people involved in horse racing, be they jockeys, breeders, trainers, stable hands or farriers. We're the best in the world at horses, without a shadow of a doubt. But we would not be the best in the world without good stallions and good mares.

To me, a good mare is like your favourite Hollywood actor – you'd know them and sort of follow their careers. There are loads of okay mares and plenty of middling mares all over the country, but finding a great mare in Ireland is like finding a pot of gold at the end of a rainbow.

Rachael Blackmore won at Cheltenham three times on a great mare called Honeysuckle – and what a brilliant name for a mare. Honeysuckle is now one of the superstar *láracha* of our generation. But I know that as I write this, in a field somewhere there's a farmer with a good mare, and she'll make great foals, and then we'll have a new champion *láir* bounding up the hill at Cheltenham come March.

19 EANÁIR / 19 JANUARY

Taos fiacla
Toothpaste

[tay-us fee-ak-la]

Is fuath liom nuair nach mbíonn taos fiacla agam san óstán.
I hate when I have no toothpaste in the hotel.

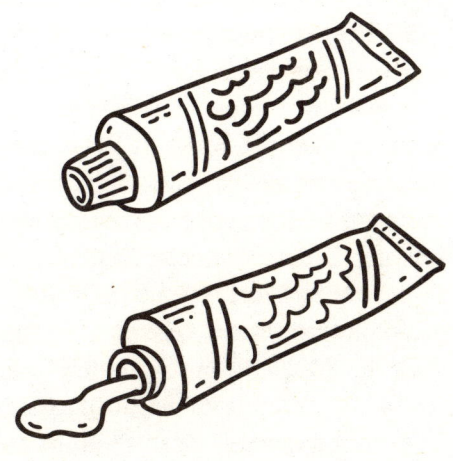

20 EANÁIR / 20 JANUARY

Gríos
Rash

[grees]

Tá gríos uafásach agam ar mo thóin.
I have a terrible rash on my bum.

When we were filming the travel show in Bali in the early 2000s, everyone seemed to be offering me cheap henna tattoos on Kuta Beach. I thought it would be a great idea to wear a sarong like David Beckham at the 1998 World Cup and finish the show by saying, 'That's it from the warm waters of Bali. We'll be in Taipei next week,' then I'd turn around, drop my sarong, and it would say '*Amú san Áise*' in henna on my white Irish arsecheeks as I ran off into the sea.

But I couldn't exactly sit there on the beach with my arse in the air while someone tattooed me. We needed somewhere private, so we parked the HiAce outside the Hard Rock Café and I bent down between two seats while a little guy called Freddie tattooed my arse for three hours in 36-degree heat. I was stressed about making sure the fadas were in the right place, so every 20 minutes Evan, the producer, would have to check the progress.

The fadas were fine and the filming was fine, but my arse was not. When we got to Taipei a few days later, my bum was so sore that I had to go to hospital. When the doctor asked me what was wrong, I dropped my pants and showed her. She took one look and said, 'Ohhhhh, not good, not good.' I said, 'I know it's not good,' because I could put my hand back and feel the red rawness of this bumpy tattoo. My whole bum had turned into an infected *gríos*. I couldn't even sit down. But I suppose it could have been worse …

21 EANÁIR / 21 JANUARY

Crann caorthainn
Rowan

[crawn cwayr-in]

Tá crann caorthainn álainn ag an ngeata.
There's a lovely rowan tree at the gate.

Rowan, the Thinker
21 JANUARY–17 FEBRUARY

I've only started learning about the significance of our Celtic horoscope and how we are connected to it – actually, to put it better, how it connects us to the Celtic world. It makes complete sense to me that we have a symbol of our land that relates to our birth dates. Trees have long been sacred to us on the island of Ireland. The druids and ancients revered them. They believed the tree was a spiritual sign of life: the roots, the trunk, the branches – symbols of the past, present and future. The druids' calendar was based on the cycles of the moon, so it's divided into 13 months, with each month represented by a different type of tree.

A new-found love of our culture is enveloping the country. We have more appreciation of the history and what this land means to us. We had friends around for dinner a while ago, and when I mentioned the Celtic tree horoscope, the conversation took off. We must have talked about it for the next hour. Everyone was so interested to learn about their tree, and I want you to know your tree too, so I've marked all the Celtic tree dates in this book.

Leo and Sagittarius and Gemini mean nothing to us, but rowan and oak and hazel are embedded deep in Irish folklore. People born of the rowan are thinkers and philosophers, they mull things over. My tree is the hazel, and when I learned this I planted one in my garden. So if you're interested, look up your Celtic tree to see what it says about you, and maybe take a trip to your garden centre to get one.

22 EANÁIR / 22 JANUARY

Luan Gorm
Blue Monday

[on loo-on gur-um]

Is seafóid cheart é Luan Gorm.
Blue Monday is a load of rubbish.

I used to present a breakfast show on 2FM, and my whole motto was 'Keep her lit'. I'd say it every day to the listeners, my Soldiers of the Dawn. We even had T-shirts made with 'KHL' on them. I was determined to be a Master of Positivity for everyone, even on Blue Monday.

This particular Luan Gorm, I was supposed to be presenting from the 2FM Roadcaster at Heuston Station in Dublin. I got up at 5 a.m. in complete darkness to walk over to the big, orange roadcaster van outside the train station. In a few hours' time, thousands of commuters from all over Ireland would descend, and I was ready to cheer them up on what was supposed to be the saddest day of the year: the third Monday in January. I think it's a load of *seafóid* (rubbish), of course – another marketing ploy to make you book a holiday – but when I got there, the roadcaster was broken down. It was so depressed on Luan Gorm that it decided to take the day off. I'm standing there ready to banish the *Luan* blues, but the big orange roadcaster was so depressed that I could do nothing about it.

23 EANÁIR / 23 JANUARY

Seachain
Watch out

[shock-in]

Seachain! Tá an sioc go dona taobh amuigh.
Watch out! There's a bad frost out there.

This word demands to be shouted; it's definitely not for your quiet voice. You can bring it out in cases of emergency – when someone is stepping off the kerb as a car approaches or they're about to wander onto an icy patch of path. *Seachain*! Watch out! It's the go-to word for a lollipop lady outside a Gaelscoil.

I wish someone had said it to me the night of the An Post Irish Book Awards in 2024, when I nearly killed myself outside the Convention Centre in Dublin. I had won an award for my first book that night and I was full of pints of Guinness that were probably only a 5 out of 10. It was a frosty night, and when my fancy black shoes hit the old wooden sleepers on that little bridge just down the way from the Convention Centre, I went flying. BANG! I whacked down on my side.

Luckily, one of the greatest hurlers of all time, Joe Canning, was holding my crystal book award, so it was safe. Joe was standing over me saying, 'Breathe, just breathe.' He's hard as nails, so when he asked if I was okay, I sort of jumped up and said, 'Yeah, yeah. I'm grand.' But I was in fucking bits. I spent the next two days covered in Voltarol, with one of those hot snakes you put in the microwave on my back.

If Joe Canning had just shouted '*Seachain!*', it would have saved me days of pain and embarrassment.

24 EANÁIR / 24 JANUARY

Leasainm
Nickname

[lass-an-im]

Tá leasainmneacha iontacha ar fud na tíre.
There are great nicknames all over the country.

Nicknames are the bedrock of any country town's sense of humour. In Navan alone, we had the Gibneys: Guggy, Nyump, Dinch, Nibbles, Pa, Buckets and Red. The Bolands: Grabber and Crumb. The Newmans: Bundles and Wimpy. The Moriartys: Flee and Fluff. The Cahills: Fly and Feather. Then there was the Rabbit Farrell, Skinner Rennicks, Spud Keelan, Apples Lally, Fishy Flanagan and Nif Chewowowow Casey, as well as lads known as Sunbeds, Teabag and Satchel. Nicknames like these are ingenious, and the people who come up with them are legends.

I suppose I have a very famous nickname. 'Shane Keogan' is on my birth cert but 'Hector Ó hEochagáin' is on my passport. Even my mother started calling me 'Hector' when I was about 12. It took her a while to get over that, but when all of our friends, neighbours, cousins, aunts and uncles were asking, 'How's Hector?', she had to say goodbye to 'Shane'.

The Irish *leasainm* is a work of art. I hope right now all of the teenagers in schools all over the country are coming up with nicknames for their friends that'll stick to them for the next 50 years.

25 EANÁIR / 25 JANUARY

Ubh bhruite
Boiled egg

[uv brich-a]

Is breá liom ubh bhruite ar maidin.
I love a boiled egg in the morning.

26 EANÁIR / 26 JANUARY

Buíocán
Egg yolk

[bwee-ok-awn]

Is breá liom nuair atá mo bhuíocán bog agus uisciúil.
I love my egg yolks soft and runny.

Is there anything better than dipping a piece of buttery toast into a soft egg yolk on a Saturday morning?

27 EANÁIR / 27 JANUARY

As mo stuaim féin
Off my own bat

[ass muh stoo-am fayn]

Rinne mé é as mo stuaim féin.
I did it off my own bat.

In the corporate world, they would say you are a 'self-starter' or that you 'have initiative', but I prefer 'off my own bat'. I don't know what bats have to do with it, but you're always proud when you do something as do stuaim féin *and can tell everyone about it.*

28 EANÁIR / 28 JANUARY

Lóistín
Accommodation

[low-shteen]

An bhfuil lóistín agat?
Do you have accommodation?

The word 'accommodation' to me says Booking.com or Trivago; it's grand for your hotel in Prague or Madrid. But *lóistín* feels like something more – it is homely, an offer of food and water and a safe place to stay. It reminds me of back in the day, when you wanted to go away for a weekend but there weren't so many hotels, so you found a little B & B or a thatched cottage for rent, or you stayed with a friend. *Lóistín* makes me think of a pot of tea and a load of sandwiches, with the fire lit and good company.

It's like when you go to a party in Galway and the craic is good, so you're still there at two in the morning, but you forgot to book accommodation, and someone says to you, '*An bhfuil lóistín agat?*' 'Do you have somewhere to lay your head? You can stay with me.' 'Accommodation' is very technical, but *lóistín* is an invitation.

29 EANÁIR / 29 JANUARY

Bruach
Bank (of a river)

[broo-ak]

Sheas an t-iascaire ar bhruach na habhann.
The fisherman stood on the bank of the river.

In Navan, we have two rivers flowing through the town: the Blackwater flows down from Lough Ramor and then meets the River Boyne in the heart of the town. You can walk for miles out of the town along the banks of the mighty river as it heads towards Slane.

30 EANÁIR / 30 JANUARY

Suathaireacht
Massage

[soo-hirr-ukt]

Ná habair gur dearbhán le haghaidh suathaireacht cinn Indiach atá ann!
Oh no, not a voucher for an Indian head massage!

Myself and Dympna have always been surrounded by friends who are into an alternative lifestyle, so we're no strangers to shiatsu, reiki, yoga and the like. I did my first yoga class about 30 years ago and I couldn't stop laughing. The teacher was from Denmark and he couldn't pronounce 'ankles'. At the end of every class, he would tell us to lie down and feel a calm come over our bodies. He'd start at our heads and work his way down, all the way to our 'angles'. I thought that would be the end of any type of meditation for me, because I was in stitches and the hour was wasted, but I still loved it.

A few years later, I was asking Dympna if she knew of anyone who did a good head massage in Galway. Like any wife would, she jumped on it and said, 'I'll get you a voucher.' Irish women love getting vouchers for their husbands. It's the box ticked when they say something they want. Bingo, job done.

I was really looking forward to the essential oils and the relaxation and emptying my head like you empty the trash bin on your computer, but from the minute I stepped in the door the massage therapist NEVER. STOPPED. TALKING. She knew everything about me and my ancestors by the time I left.

My head was absolutely wrecked. I would have done a better job just scratching my head myself. I'll do all the acupuncture and sauna and Wim Hof sessions, but never, ever give me a voucher for a head massage.

31 EANÁIR / 31 JANUARY

Ceannródaí
Trailblazer

[kyaun row-dee]

Cé hiad na ceannródaithe i do pharóiste?
Who are the trailblazers in your parish?

I love the word *ceannródaí*, and even in English it's cool. It makes me think of a cowboy on horseback, dust being kicked up as he rides through the Wild West looking for opportunity. He's gone to the New World to make a new life – he's blazing a trail.

The person I automatically think of when I hear *ceannródaí* is Richie Ball, my English teacher in secondary school. We never knew what to expect when he'd walk into class. He could say, 'Put the books away, let's do an improvisation', and we'd all just have to go with the flow. I remember him saying to us, 'Okay, I won't do poetry today if anyone can come up here and beat me in press-ups.' Then he'd get down and do about 50 press-ups. We'd never beat him and we were all mad for poetry by the end of it. He was an innovator in the way he taught us English.

You don't have to run a big company or be a multimillionaire to be a trailblazer. They're the unsung heroes in your community, the people raising thousands for breast cancer, running local Men's Sheds or pushing for change for the good of everyone in the parish. Michael D. Higgins was a trailblazer because he came up with the idea of having an Irish-speaking TV channel. TG4 was launched with festivity and fireworks in 1996, and where would we be without it? I hope my sons are trailblazers with their friends. So when you hear the word *ceannródaí*, I want you to think of the trailblazers in your life. They should be celebrated.

1 FEABHRA / 1 FEBRUARY

Imbolg

[im-bull-ug]

Tá an bhliain nua tagtha; seo Imbolg.
The new year is upon us; this is Imbolg.

Winter solstice has passed and the spring equinox is on the horizon. The land is awakening from its slumber. The sky is opening up. It's the start of something new. Imbolg is upon us. Doesn't Imbolg sound beautiful? It's a word carved from our land. It's ritualistic, it's powerful, it's tribal, and now more than ever, people all over the country are turning back to Mother Earth.

The first day in February marks the start of spring in Ireland, and our ancestors celebrated it with the festival of Imbolg. It's the promise of something new after months of darkness – you notice the stretch in the day and the daffodils are just poking their heads above ground.

I don't really know the origins of this old Irish word, but I like to split it into two and think of it as *im* plus *bolg*: 'butter belly'. I imagine one of Fionn Mac Cumhaill's gang was nicknamed Butterbelly. A great warrior of the Fianna, a proper *scorach* (big, tall man) who was fierce in battle, but because he was born on 1 February his friends called him Butterbelly.

Now 1 February is St Brigid's Day and we get a day off work. Brigid used to be a pagan goddess until the Christians claimed her, so what might have been a huge party to mark the start of spring in pagan times is now celebrated by a load of schoolchildren struggling to make crosses out of rushes.

2 FEABHRA / 2 FEBRUARY

Imleacán
Bellybutton

[im-la-kawn]

Cén saghas imleacáin atá agat?
What sort of bellybutton have you?

Inny, outty, horizontal, vertical, closed, open – an *imleacán* comes in all sizes and forms. I have an inny, a small cavern. Navan is 'An Uaimh' in Irish, which means 'The Cave', and my bellybutton is the same. There could be a little squirrel hiding in there.

I was fascinated with keeping my bellybutton clean as a child. Small bits of cotton from those white vests you wore in the 1970s always got in, and I'd spend my time in the bath fishing out the fluff. Even now if I'm at the gym, I could be standing in the changing room after a sauna, bollock naked, checking my bellybutton for fluff.

We take them for granted. Bellybuttons are the nozzles of life. Everything comes through that umbilical cord from Mammy: oxygen, blood, nutrients, a half a glass of white wine. Then as soon as we're out of the womb, we cut it. I was at the births of my boys and I got to cut the cords, but I didn't realise it was a serious piece of kit. You think it's going to be like a ribbon-cutting ceremony, but 60 seconds later you're still there trying to get through it. You're standing there holding the scissors, and the cord is going, 'I am life. You don't get to snip me away so quickly.'

Imleacáin are so important to us in the womb; then we spend the rest of our lives covering them up.

3 FEABHRA / 3 FEBRUARY

Scornach
Throat

[score-nock]

A *Mhamaí, tá mo scornach tinn.*
Mammy, I have a sore throat.

Today is St Blaise's Day, the time of sore throats. I was scalded by tonsillitis year after year as a child. My mother, Trina, would check the glands and say, 'Oh, they're like golf balls,' and I'd get a day off school. Some of my friends got their tonsils out and never looked back, but I had no such luck.

Instead, me and my brothers were trotted down to St Mary's Church in town, a big, grey building off the main street. We'd kneel down at the altar waiting for the priest to come up with his two holy candles crossed in an X shape and hold them against our throats to bless us. I can still see Trina sitting behind the first pew thinking, 'I love this.' In fairness to her, I'd come out of the church and my throat golf balls would be gone.

St Blaise's prayer is supposed to keep your throat healthy so you can talk correctly and sing praises to God. So now I can talk correctly and use my voice to record podcasts and the like.

4 FEABHRA / 4 FEBRUARY

Cnámh smiolgadáin
Collarbone

[keh-nawv smeel-guh-dawn]

Bhris an marcach Davy Russell a chnámh smiolgadáin cúig huaire.
The jockey Davy Russell broke his collar bone five times.

Jockeys break collarbones like there's no tomorrow. They're hurtling along at 30 miles an hour on a half-tonne animal, jumping fences, and in the blink of an eye they're thrown from the saddle like they're in an ejector seat. Crash, bang, wallop. Ruptured spleen, dislocated shoulder, broken collarbone.

The GAA breaks collarbones too. You'll see it standing on the sideline of any game:

'What's wrong with Paul?'

'He's done his collarbone.'

'Right, get him off the field so.'

We've all seen that image of a player, no matter what age or level, coming off the pitch with the jersey pulled up over their arm to support the break. A broken collarbone is one of the great Irish injuries of the sports fields.

Broc
Badger

[bruck]

Ní fheicimid an broc rómhinic, ach bíonn sé i gcónaí thart.
We don't see the badger much, but he's always around.

6 FEABHRA / 6 FEBRUARY

Boladh
Smell

[bull-ah]

Cén boladh is fearr leat?
What's your favourite smell?

Where did the word 'smell' come from? It almost sounds German. *Boladh* is a far more interesting word. It's when your nose goes, 'Is that the dinner on?'

When we were shooting the travel series in Central America, we finished in Belize. The bags were packed and we were ready for home. But first we had to get there. We took a two-hour boat ride across the Bay of Honduras back to Belize City and hopped on a four-hour flight to Atlanta. We had a five-hour stopover there before taking a night flight to Newark; then we went from Newark to Heathrow and from Heathrow to Dublin. The last leg of the journey was Burkes Bus to Galway.

Forty-three hours after leaving Belize, I was the last one off the bus as it pulled into the station in Galway, and I'll never forget it. The driver turned to me and said, 'How are you, Hector? Are you going home?' 'I am,' I replied. 'Sure I'm going that way anyway – I'll drop you at the head of the road.' The 'head' of the road, right at the top – what a beautiful country phrase!

It was after midnight on a gorgeous summer's evening, and when the doors opened with that pneumatic 'pssssshhhhh' sound, the smell of the countryside hit me. It was warm and balmy and as I walked down my laneway, I could smell summer in the fields all around me. After filming in all of those amazing countries, I thought, 'There's nowhere else like this in the world.' It was the *boladh* of home.

7 FEABHRA / 7 FEBRUARY

Foraois
Forest

[furr-eesh]

Déan cinnte go bhfuil a fhios agat cá bhfuil d'fhoraois áitúil.
Make sure you know where your local forest is.

I've used *foraois* so much over the last few years because we've been going deeper into jungles for the TV show. It was a new word for me until recently, and I want to share it, because a lot of people will know that the word for 'wood' is *coill*, but you could be in and out of a *coill* in half an hour. *Foraois* is the word you need for miles and miles of huge trees, the kind you find in Nova Scotia in Canada. I saw the most amazing forest in Latvia. It was the middle of winter, snow everywhere, and we were driving deep into one of the biggest forests in the country, where trees are felled and the wood is shipped all over Europe to build houses. All I could see out the window for about five hours was dense forest: swathes of spruce trees that went on forever.

My favourite local forest is Knockmaa. It's nothing like the forests of Latvia or Canada, but what it lacks in size it makes up for in myth. Legend has it that Queen Maeve is buried there, and it was also the home of Finnbheara, the fairy king of Connacht. The forest is like the Electric Picnic for fairies. Children have put down hundreds of those little fairy houses all over the forest, and it's just a magical place.

So you can use *coill* when you're walking your dog through your small local wood – you wouldn't get lost there – but you'd better be prepared when you're going into a *foraois*.

8 FEABHRA / 8 FEBRUARY

Dufair
Jungle

[duff-er]

Thosaigh an bháisteach ag titim go trom sa dufair.
The rain started to fall heavily in the jungle.

Visiting the Serengeti is like going back to the source of all life. To see the migration of thousands of zebras, herds of elephants in the distance, and hear the roars of lions and howling of hyenas is truly remarkable. Even the warthogs would steal your boots if you left them outside your tent.

In the middle of the vast savannah is the Ngorongoro Crater, and we camped there for three days. It is a volcanic caldera, full of dense woodland and jungle life. At night-time, me, Rosco and my producer Evan would all pile into one tent together because we were shitting it. I'd need to pee at about one in the morning and I'd ask the lads to come with me, but Evan would be snoring and Rosco would just give out and tell me to go back to sleep. I'd zip open the tent and there would be a man sitting there holding an AK-47, guarding us from lions. I'd ask if everything was okay and he'd reply, 'No problem, sir,' cool as anything. Then when you're standing there staring into the Serengeti having a wee, all you can hear are the sounds of the jungle.

Dufair is a new enough word for me, so it feels strange to say. We write up the voiceovers for the TG4 show in English and send them off to a special translation laboratory in the West of Ireland where Irish-language scientists translate it. It's crazy to think I went all the way to Tanzania to learn *dufair*, but that's the beauty of the travel show – new countries mean new words. I don't know every Irish word, so these language scientists have given me loads of new ones over the years. And now it's in your Irish arsenal, so you'll be trying to find ways of dropping *dufair* into your chats *as Gaeilge* to show it off.

9 FEABHRA / 9 FEBRUARY

Guth
Voice

[guh]

Tá guth álainn aici.
She has a lovely voice.

Guth *is a nicer word for voice than* glór. Guth *is that voice that really stands out, the one you love as soon as you hear it. A* guth *stops you in your tracks.*

10 FEABHRA / 10 FEBRUARY

Imní
Worry

[im-nee]

Tá imní orm – beidh mo thástáil tiomána agam inniu.
I'm worried – I've got my driving test today.

Imní *is the feeling of 'Fuck, something's wrong'. You get it before an exam, before your driving test, before a job interview. It's a bad sort of feeling that you can't shake.*

11 FEABHRA / 11 FEBRUARY

Nocht
Naked

[nukht]

Níl muid rómhaith le cúrsaí nochtachta sa tír seo.
We're not very good about being naked in this country.

This is like my very own episode of the show *Naked and Afraid: Nocht agus Faiteach*. I was drinking Budvar on an empty stomach at a Christmas party all evening in Dublin. I had also met some mates before the party just to get a good run at it, you know yourself ... So at about one in the morning, everything started to get a bit too wobbly, and I got a taxi to the Beacon Hotel, where I was staying the night.

I was *caochta* – ossified. I can't even remember getting into bed. I woke up a while later to go to the toilet, but everything was dark, so I couldn't see well. I was fighting the helicopters when my hand landed on a handle. The door felt oddly heavy, but I pulled it open and walked through. It closed behind me with a click, and I realised I was in a dark corridor. Now, I sleep naked, so I'm buck *nocht* and locked out of my room.

I made my way towards a dim light at the end of the corridor. It was coming from an industrial lift used by the staff. I got in and started pressing buttons, and a voice said, 'Hello? Are you alright?' 'Where am I?' I asked. 'This is the service line. I'm in Cork and you're in a lift in a hotel in Dublin.'

Next minute the doors closed and the lift started to go down. I'm thinking, 'WTF, is this the end of my career?' The doors opened and I headed out onto Sandyford Road, cars zooming by, and I hid behind a bush and managed to get the attention of a bouncer, who let me back in. The shame of it was so bad that I got up at six in the morning to flee the scene. We are not good at being *nocht* in Ireland, and I'm a prime example of that.

12 FEABHRA / 12 FEBRUARY

Nóinín
Daisy

[no-neen]

Bhí an gairdín lán de nóiníní.
The garden was full of daisies.

Daisies have to be one of our most recognisable small flowers. They find their home in fields and paddocks and gardens and parks and pathways. The shape and colour of a nóinín *is known to us all; it brings to mind memories of childhood garden adventures, the long summer days playing on the lawns of the country.*

13 FEBRUARY / 13 FEABHRA

Buacaire
Tap

[boo-ca-ra]

D'fhág tú an buacaire ar siúl an oíche ar fad.
You left the tap on all night.

14 FEABHRA / 14 FEBRUARY
Lá Fhéile Vailintín / Valentine's Day

A thaisce
My love/my treasure

[a hash-ka]

Fuair mé bláthanna duit, a thaisce.
I got you flowers, my love.

There are so many ways to say 'my love' in Irish; we're big on grá. You can throw a thaisce *in at the end of a sentence to reinforce your appreciation for that person.*

15 FEABHRA / 15 FEBRUARY

Braillíní
Sheets

[braw-lee-nee]

Ná déan dearmad na braillíní a chur amach ar an líne.
Don't forget to put the sheets out on the line.

Is there any more of a treat than getting into bed having put on fresh sheets? The word *braillíní* makes me think of throwing sheets in the air after you take them off the line, the smell of fresh wind and fabric softener wafting from them.

I always try to fold the sheets with my wife. Sometimes she'll come in while me and our boys are on the couch watching the Champions League and she'll dump about 500 pairs of white socks on us to sort out. But I'll always jump up to fold the sheets with her, because I want my boys to see that it's teamwork.

In most Irish households, when the sheets come off the line and into the kitchen, they might sit there for two hours before they're moved. They get stuck on step three in the logistics of washing: step one is getting them washed, two is putting them out to dry, three is bringing them inside for organisation and distribution, four is transporting them upstairs to their destination.

There are special *braillíní* too – the ones your mother puts on the bed when you're coming home for the weekend, or the ones that only come out over Christmas. Then there's the lovely feeling of brushed cotton sheets in the winter when it's cold. But the biggest treat of all is when your better half says, 'I changed the sheets today.' These are special moments in Irish sheet life.

16 FEABHRA / 16 FEBRUARY

Ar dualgas
On duty

[air dool-gus]

Bhí an garda ar dualgas aréir sa bhaile mór.
The garda was on duty last night in the town.

I was stopped at traffic lights by a Gaelscoil one December morning. It was a lovely crisp winter's day. The sun was out and it was nippy but dry, so all the kids were out in the yard. The place was teeming with activity, and in the middle of all of the chaos there was a teacher walking around with a big smile on her face. And you know if the teacher is happy, then the kids are happy. All of her colleagues were probably inside having a sandwich and a cup of tea, but she was *ar dualgas* for today.

I did the same for years when I was a *cúntóir* in Coláiste na bhFiann in St Mel's College in Longford. I'd be on night duty in the boys' dormitory, which was Dorm B. It was lights out at 10.30 p.m., no question, and I loved to have the craic with the students, so I came up with a rhyme that I'd say every night. I'd hit the switch on the dorm wall and hear the little chats still going on, so I'd say: '*Ciúnas sa suanlios*' (Quiet in the dormitory). And about a hundred young lads would reply, '*B na mbuachaillí – agus SIN É!*' (B boys, and that's it). On a quiet night, all the boys would be asleep by 11, but you'd still have to stay up until midnight before you could hit the hay if you were *ar dualgas*.

I haven't thought about that rhyme since about 1986, and the memory has put a smile on my face like that teacher on yard duty in the Gaelscoil.

17 FEABHRA / 17 FEBRUARY

Ceapaire
Sandwich

[kyap-ir-a]

An stopfaimid le hagaidh ceapaire ar an mbealach?
Will we stop for a sandwich on the way?

We've come a long way to get to chicken fillet rolls with a bit of chipotle sauce. Back in my school days, we had a choice of two sandwiches for lunch: it was the classic sliced corned beef one week and Sandwich Spread the next.

Sandwich Spread tasted like it sounded. It looked like diced carrots, onions and peppers mixed with mayonnaise. I'd say it was invented in the UK in the 1970s by the same people who invented Branston Pickle.

'We'll put in carrots and onions and mayonnaise and they'll fucking love it.'

'What will we call it?'

'I dunno, Sandwich Spread?'

It was genius and horrific at the same time.

Now my go-to *ceapaire* is a tuna cheese melt with red onion, sliced green pickles, lettuce and tomato on honey-and-oat bread. Whenever myself, Rosco and Evan pass a Subway on our travels, we always stop and pile into the place to get a *ceapaire*. It's the same in Indonesia as it is in Alabama. Sandwiches always taste better when you're on your way somewhere, as long as the filling isn't Sandwich Spread.

18 FEABHRA / 18 FEBRUARY

Fuinseog
Ash

[fwin-showg]

Tá fadhb mhór againn sa tír seo le galar na bhfuinseog, críonadh siar fuinseoige.
We have a big problem in this country with the ash tree disease, ash dieback.

Ash, the Enchanter
18 FEBRUARY–17 MARCH

Ash is your Celtic tree if you were born this time of year. You are the dreamers of the group, off in your own world like the little helicopter seeds that spin off ash trees. It's a standout tree of the forest, immense and old and full of enlightenment. I think the ancient wizards of our land, the druids, made their wands from the ash tree, wielding power and magic and knowledge. If there were a tree this island was built on, it would be the mighty ash.

19 FEABHRA / 19 FEBRUARY

Duilleog labhrais
Bay leaf

[dill-owg lau-rish]

Tá crann duilleog labhrais agam taobh amuigh do mo dhoras tosaigh.
I have a bay leaf tree outside my front door.

20 FEABHRA / 20 FEBRUARY

Siar

(Go) back, westwards

[sheer]

An bhfuil tú ag dul siar le haghaidh na Nollag?
Are you going back (west) for Christmas?

This is one of the most brilliant, small words you can have in any language. It's vital. We love 'going back' (to) places. You can use it for going back over a book or moving back on a football pitch or going back to a place.

This is pure Connemara altogether, because *siar* specifically means to go back west. To cross the Shannon. To go back home. You can only really use it if you're from the West of Ireland, because if you never lived there you can't really go back to it.

We're a nation of emigrants, so the idea of 'going back' is in our DNA, and *siar* is a word full of movement. You can't use it when you're talking about standing at the back of the class or the back of a queue. That 'back' is '*cúl*'. *Siar* is the one for when you see someone stuck in a tricky spot in a car park in Connemara and you're helping them reverse: 'Go back. Back a bit further. There you have it.' *Siar* has trajectory.

21 FEABHRA / 21 FEBRUARY

Aniar

(Come from the) west

[an-eer]

Tháinig mo chol ceathar aniar as Conamara le haghaidh na bainise.
My cousin came from Connemara for the wedding.

You learned *siar* yesterday, so now I'm giving you *aniar* to keep in your back pocket. These are common words in Connemara, but we're getting a bit tricky. *Aniar* is to come from the west. If you have a friend from Connemara and they're coming to Meath to see you, they have to physically come *aniar* on their visit. It's a west-to-east trip, a journey from one side of the country to another, with Connemara remaining the focal point for their orientation.

It's a technical term, but it's useful when you're making that cross-country journey. *Siar* and *aniar* are lovely little bridges of words across the stream of conversation *as Gaeilge*. And I have another one for you tomorrow …

22 FEABHRA / 22 FEBRUARY

Anall
From over there

[an-awl]

Tháinig mo chlann anall ó Mhanchain don samhradh.
My family came home from Manchester for the summer.

---

*A**nall* has strong connotations of coming home from 'out foreign'; travelling home over vast water. This word was formed deep in the west of County Galway from decades and decades of emigration: fathers leaving to get construction work in England, families heading to Boston for a new life, sons and daughters moving to Australia for the better cost of living. They are sad and hard times, but then there's always the happiness of being able to return home, to come *anall*.

You can also use *anall* if you're in a large crowd – at a concert or a céilí or a function room full of people – when someone walks across to you: *Tháinig sé anall* (He walked across).

23 FEABHRA / 23 FEBRUARY

Breis
More (distance)

[bresh]

Rinne sé breis is 70 míle ar an rothar inné.
He did over 70 miles on the bike yesterday.

Breis *is for the long-distance runner who's done 20 miles and pushes for five more, or the extra hour you need to spend on a project to get it finished. It's a word for measurement; you would never use it for food or drink: 'Would you like extra wine?' is passive-aggressive.*

24 FEABHRA / 24 FEBRUARY

Tuilleadh
More (extra)

[till-a]

An bhfuil tuilleadh prátaí uait?
Would you like more potatoes?

Tuilleadh can be used for more anything – more food, more rain, more information: *Tuilleadh eolais ar fáil ag ...* (More information can be found at ...). It's the word you need when *breis* (more, p. 60) won't do.

I learned *tuilleadh* quickly in the Gaeltacht, because when the *bean an tí* says to you every day for three weeks, 'Would you like more potatoes, more spaghetti, more chips, more tea, more toast?' you have to know what she's talking about or you'll miss out on the second helpings.

It's the classic at an Irish wedding when the servers go around the tables offering more veg and potatoes. The couple getting married could have spent fifty grand on their big day, but if you aren't offered *tuilleadh* potatoes or *tuilleadh* wine, you'll say the wedding was shite.

25 FEABHRA / 25 FEBRUARY

Torann
Noise

[tur-ann]

Thit muid inár gcodladh ar an trá agus muid ag éisteacht le torann na farraige.
We fell asleep on the beach listening to the sound of the sea.

It's the dead of night and you hear a noise. You lift your head off the pillow and wait for the sound – maybe it's the door banging or the lid of the bin flapping outside. It's a fright in the silence. It's a torann.

26 FEABHRA / 26 FEBRUARY

Ó thuaidh; Ó dheas
Up north; Down south

[o hoo-a]; [o yas]

Tá an pheil Ghaelach an-láidir anois ó thuaidh.
The football up north now is very strong.

Tá an saol ó dheas go hálainn, go mór mór in Iarthar Chorcaí.
The life down south is beautiful, especially in West Cork.

27 FEABHRA / 27 FEBRUARY

Teocht
Temperature

[chow-akht]

Tá do theocht ard, a stór.
You have a high temperature, my darling.

For anyone who has had children, you know that *teocht* is the word you don't want to hear.
'Did you check his temperature there? Is it high?'
'Yeah, 39 degrees.'
'Right, I'll get the Calpol.'
Those were the days. The best gadget we ever got as parents of young children was that little nozzle you stick in their ears – beep and the temperature comes up. We swore by it. We still have it. We're well past the Calpol days, but the odd time you would find a bottle at the back of a press and it would bring you right back to the teething and the chesty coughs.

Make sure to use *teocht* on your *laethanta saoire* (holidays) as well. We think we're used to heat and cold in Ireland, but we're not. You'll be looking forward to a bit of heat on your two weeks in Alicante, but as soon as you walk down the stairs off the plane with your winter coat over your arm, you'll say 'Jesus Christ, I'm too warm.'

When I got back from Siberia, this aul lad in the local pub asked me how I got on. When I told him it was −32 Celsius, he said, 'Would you stop. Sure that's nothing. That's a dry cold.' But if the temperature in Ireland goes down to −4, the country shuts down. We like to think we're grand with the extreme *teochtaí*, but we're not.

28 FEABHRA / 28 FEBRUARY

Mangach
Pollock

[mawn-goch]

Bhí spotaí speisialta le haghaidh na mangach ar an taobh eile den oileán.
There were special spots for the pollock on the other side of the island.

I love the sound of this word – it's just lovely to pronounce. It's not a word you would use regularly on Main Street in Galway, but on Inis Meáin it's ingrained in daily conversation. There's an ecosystem of Irish words used that you would never hear on the mainland. The waters surrounding the island are abundant. People on the island talk about fish the way city dwellers talk about traffic.

I learned *mangach* when I lived on Inis Meáin in the early 1990s and it's stayed with me since. Knowing it and saying it gave me a bit of self-assurance about my ability to converse with the locals. Like I would see a currach come in down at the pier and be able to say to the fishermen:

'*Céard atá agaibh?*' (What have you got?)

'*Mangachaigh, Hector. Cúpla mangach.*' (Pollock, Hector. A couple of pollock.)

On Inis Meáin, fish is always on the menu for dinner and it's always on the menu in conversations. It's part of island life.

29 FEABHRA / 29 FEBRUARY
Bliain bhisigh / Leap Year

Bliain bhisigh
Leap year

[blee-an vish-ig]

Tarlaíonn bliain bhisigh gach ceithre bliana.
A leap year happens every four years.

I put this in for all the poor unfortunates who have their birthdays on 29 February. You can celebrate your birthday on the day you were born exactly every four years, because for the other three years your birthday disappears into a black hole of time. Only Professor Brian Cox can solve this problem.

1 MÁRTA / 1 MARCH

Seift
A plan

[sheft]

Bhí seift aige conas fáil isteach go dtí an fhéile gan íoc.
He had a plan for how to get into the festival for free.

Seift is a dynamic little word that's all about the game plan. Better yet, it's a masterplan – something that took time to come up with and execute to perfection.

I used to get 'triple-A' passes to Electric Picnic back when it was run by Aiken Promotions, when the Picnic was the Picnic – I was 'Access All Areas'. So I was the man on the inside when we came up with a *seift* to sneak my friends in late on a Friday night.

At about 10 p.m. under the cover of darkness, I would head out of the festival to my car with a load of high-vis vests and pick up the lads. They'd put on the jackets and pile into the car. Now, the key to coming into a festival with a carload of lads is to drive up to the crew gate really slowly with the window rolled down, ready to engage. Then the arm goes out the window and I say, 'Well, boys?' There's no music pumping, no chatting, all the lads in the car look like they're back from a break. And then … 'How's it going, Hector? On you go, on you go.' And we're in.

We park the car, take off the high-vis jackets, crack the boot open and take out the beers, and then we hug each other. Now that's what you call a *seift*. There's no real harm in it, it's not a bad thing – it's just a bit of ingenuity and bravado.

2 MÁRTA / 2 MARCH

Sruth
Current

[shruh]

Bhí sruth an-láidir san abhainn ón uisce ag teacht ón sliabh.
There was a strong current in the river from the water coming off the mountain.

Sruth is that beautiful movement of water, the power of a river winding through a bog or a forest or a mountain. You can almost hear the water running through the word: *sruth*.

There's a small fishing hut beside a river next to a road in Connemara – I think it's called Gillie's Hut – and every time I pass it, I have to stop the car and get out. I stand there in awe of the absolute beauty of the place. There's a small waterfall, the river is wild and clear, and the fishing hut is like something out of a movie – a small, whitewashed stone cottage with a thatched roof.

The air is fresh, the water is pure and it is surrounded by mountains. It is about three miles from Maam Cross on the road back towards Ros Muc in County Galway, but it looks like it could be in Switzerland. Water flows from little tributaries to join the river and the sound of the *sruth* is everywhere.

3 MÁRTA / 3 MARCH

Aontú
Agreement

[ain-too]

Bhí aontú idir an dá thaobh aréir.
There was an agreement between the two sides last night.

An agreement, an alliance, a coming together. Aontú is used by trade unions and student unions alike all over the country.

4 MÁRTA / 4 MARCH

Easpa
Lack

[ah-spa]

Bhí easpa bia sa chuisneoir.
There was a lack of food in the fridge.

Easpa means a shortage of something – it could be food, money or effort. It can be used at half-time in the dressing room when the team isn't performing: 'Come on, boys. There's been a lack of effort on the pitch.' Unfortunately we say it a lot in this country: there's an *easpa* of hospital beds, houses, teachers, nurses, doctors, tilers and plumbers.

We've all experienced *easpa* when we get home after a long weekend away. We open the fridge and all that's there is two Petit Filous. There's nothing sorrier than an empty fridge when you're only in the door after three hours on the plane and two hours in the car. When you're heading home from the airport after a holiday, if you at least pick up a pint of milk, you know there'll be no *easpa bainne* and you can make a cup of tea.

5 MÁRTA / 5 MARCH

Géarghá
A real need

[gair ghaw]

Tá géarghá le droichead nua i gcathair na Gaillimhe.
There's a real need for a new bridge in Galway city.

Galway city has to be the biggest bottleneck in Europe. From seven every morning, there are thousands of cars trying to get over one single bridge. You'd get through Mumbai or Manchester quicker than you would Galway on a Friday afternoon, too. If you're reading this and you're from Galway, you'll know what I mean; there's a real need for another bridge.

How many times do you hear some minister or spokesperson on the *Nuacht* on TG4 saying, '*Tá géarghá le hathrú*' (There's a real need for change)? I can hear it in that politician's voice. Some of them are fluent, some of them are trying to get better, and some of them are plain aul shite *as Gaeilge*. If I was a politician's aide prepping them for their next public interview in Irish, I'd be ramming *géarghá* into their skulls while they're hurtling down the motorway in the back of the BMW. 'Now, Minister, before you cut the ribbon to open the new server farm, don't forget to get this phrase in there. *Géarghá, géarghááááá.*' *Géarghá* is a politician's wet dream.

6 MÁRTA / 6 MARCH

Ordóg
Thumb

[ur-dowg]

Stop mé ag diúl ar m'ordóg nuair a bhí mé a dó dhéag.
I stopped sucking my thumb when I was 12.

7 MÁRTA / 7 MARCH

Ingne
Nails (on hands or toes)

[ing-nah]

Bhí an buachaill óg ag ithe a ingne gach lá.
The young boy was eating his nails every day.

My youngest lad bites his nails. Like a lot of parents in the same situation, we've asked him to stop, told him to stop, bribed him to stop, gave up trying to get him to stop, bought him that little bottle of manky varnish to put on them to make him stop ... alas, he still bites his nails.

When I was 12 years old and wouldn't stop sucking my thumb, my father came up with a plan. He marched me out to the fields where the cattle were grazing, found a fresh cow pat – soft and pungent, only a few hours old – and he grabbed my thumb and stuck it deep into the heart of it. He held my thumb tight as I cried and asked him to let it go, but he didn't. He held it there for long enough that I couldn't fully get rid of the smell for ages, but by then the job was done. I never dreamed of putting my thumb back in my mouth ever again. Me and my youngest boy will be heading down to the field soon ...

8 MÁRTA / 8 MARCH

Coincheap
Brainwave/concept

[cun-cyap]

Bhí coincheap againn conas lá saor a fháil ón scoil.
We had a brainwave about how to get a day off school.

Coincheap is a bit of a technical word. You wouldn't be using it every day, but you know when you need it. It's for those brainwaves you have or you come across: the initial idea, the beginning of the project, the eureka moment.

Coincheap makes me think of seeing a red-headed lad from a school in Limerick on the news back in 2005 having won the Young Scientist of the Year award at the age of 16. He had a *coincheap*, worked hard, and then went on with his brother to co-found Stripe – one of the biggest global online payment companies.

One of my favourite *coincheaps* is the invention of the firelog. We've come a long way from the traditional firelighter. On top of that, I'm very smart with firelogs. I get my big, serrated knife and I cut them into three mini firelogs, so you get three fires for the price of one. It's a brainwave on top of a brainwave. A *coincheap* on a *coincheap*.

9 MÁRTA / 9 MARCH

T-léine
T-shirt

[tee layna]

Tá T-léine agam ó cheolchoirm na Stone Roses i gCorcaigh.
I've a T-shirt from a Stone Roses concert in Cork.

I'm a T-léine *man and I was a* T-léine *boy. They're more than just pieces of clothing. Our favourite ones remind us of a gig, a holiday, a special moment in life. Cool* T-léinte *are always cool. Keep them, cherish them and remember the good days you had wearing them.*

10 MÁRTA / 10 MARCH

Suasóg
Yuppie

[soos-owg]

An bhfuil suasóg ar bith fágtha sa tír seo?
Are there any yuppies left in this country?

We all know a yuppie – collar up, deck shoes, a bit of a Ross O'Carroll-Kelly. This word was created in the 1980s. Suasóga *are a dying breed.*

11 MÁRTA / 11 MARCH

Bodóg
Heifer

[bud-owg]

Bhí an bhodóg ina seasamh ina haonar sa pháirc.
The heifer stood alone in the field.

My uncles and aunts were all massive farmers. It was a big business for them. My father ran a drapery shop in town, but he always had to have a *bodóg* or two, or a few calves that we would buy at the mart over in Carnaross. The field at the back of the house was small, with just a little shed, but it was ours. We were mini farmers.

The bull arriving to do his job was big news in the area. The water diviner would arrive with his hazel rods to find springs all around. I'd pull a calf with my father on freezing winter nights. These were great things to be exposed to at the age of seven or eight. All around me were rich green fields and good land. We only lived a mile and a half from town, but it was pure countryside.

12 MÁRTA / 12 MARCH

Searrach bliana
Yearling foal

[sharr-ak bleen-eh]

Bhí na díolacháin searrach bliana ar siúl an tseachtain seo caite i dTigh na Sióg.
The yearling sales were on in Fairyhouse last week.

There's a massive pot of horses in Ireland and throughout the year, depending on what month it is, there'll be a big sale. You could have a mare sale, a stallion sale, a horses in training sale, a national hunt sale, even a breeze-up sale (two-year-old horses who haven't been raced). You also have foal sales – the babies – and a year later, those foals will be sold at yearling sales. This is where the one-year-old horses are bought and go off to secondary school to become the stars of horse racing.

Some people are experts in buying yearlings. They bring them back to their farms, mind them, breed them, train them, build up their physiques and a year or two later they bring them back to market to sell them on so these horses can embark on their careers.

You could buy a pony for your son or daughter in Spancelhill or you could spend a million quid in the blink of an eye at Goffs. But no matter what level, we have the best *searraigh bhliana* in the world in Ireland.

13 MÁRTA / 13 MARCH

Doirt
To spill

[durch]

Dhoirt sé an t-uisce ar fad ar an urlár.
He spilled all the water on the floor.

It's that basin of dirty water slipping out of your hands, the litre of milk you drop on the kitchen floor or the tanker you see on the news that's spilling oil into the ocean.

14 MÁRTA / 14 MARCH

Breac
Trout

[brack]

Bhí breac úr agam aréir don dinnéar.
I had fresh trout last night for dinner.

15 MÁRTA / 15 MARCH

Ar an drabhlás
On a session

[er on drow-lawss]

Chuaigh na leaideanna amach ar an drabhlás Lá 'le Stiofáin ar fad.
The lads went on a right session the whole of St Stephen's Day.

Whether you're doing a solid day's drinking deep in the hills of Baile Bhuirne in Cork, doing the rounds of the pubs with the lads after watching a match in Galway, or day-drinking in Dublin, you're *ar an drabhlás*.

A lad called Daithí taught me this phrase. He was as Dublin as the Dodder River, but when he spoke Irish it was like a time machine that transported me back to the olden days in West Cork. He spoke English in a Dublin accent, but when he spoke Irish, it was in the most majestic Munster dialect. He had a deep love and boundless knowledge of it.

We would sit in places like Cultúrlann na hÉireann in Monkstown – an Irish-speaking *tearmann* (sanctuary, p. 22) in the middle of south Dublin – sipping creamy pints, listening to traditional tunes. When he told me we were *ar an drabhlás*, I could hear the phrase echo around the valleys of Cork.

16 MÁRTA / 16 MARCH

Scaoil amach do shamhlaíocht
Let your imagination go

[skweel amok duh how-lee-ukt]

Lig do scíth, dún do shúile agus scaoil amach do shamhlaíocht.
Relax, close your eyes and let your imagination go.

If there had been an imagination class in school, I would have got an A1. Some kids in school do it all the time. A lot are punished for it, but I champion it – it's what our minds are built for. I like looking out windows, daydreaming, letting my mind chill out and open up.

If I were the Minister for Education, I'd put it on the school curriculum. Imagine a *Rang Samhlaíochta*, an Imagination Class:

'I teach Maths – what do you teach?'

'I teach Imagination.'

It would be unbelievable if we encouraged it in school. Our imaginations are an amazing gift. We don't daydream and let our minds drift as much as we should. And we shouldn't underestimate the daydreamers. We're not a literary nation for nothing – they could be the next Irish winner of the Nobel Prize for Literature.

17 MÁRTA / 17 MARCH
Lá Fhéile Pádraig / St Patrick's Day

Paráid
Parade

[par-awj]

Tá clú agus cáil ar Pharáid Lá 'le Pádraig ar fud an domhain.
The St Patrick's Day Parade is famous all over the world.

One of my favourite moments of all the series of the TG4 travel show happened on 17 March 2018 in Kathmandu, Nepal. While we were there, we heard there was a brand-new Irish pub opening, and the lady from Cork and her Nepalese husband who owned it were running around frantically trying to get the place ready for St Patrick's Day.

After a beer and a chat, we found out that Kathmandu was probably the only capital city in the world that didn't have a Paddy's Day parade, so we said we would organise one ourselves.

Twenty-four hours later, at 3 p.m. on 17 March, we were walking down one of the main streets in Kathmandu holding a five-foot leprechaun mounted on a pole. He was like a Hindu god, an Irish Ganesh with a ginger beard and a green hat.

Word got around and people joined the *paráid*. Then I started chanting '*Namaste!* St Patrick's Day!' on a loudspeaker and Irish people were spilling out of cafés and hostels – it was like a call to prayer for people in Irish sports jerseys. It was a savage afternoon altogether and, even better, later that day back in the newest Irish pub in Nepal, we watched Ireland beat England in the Six Nations in Twickenham. *Namaste*.

18 MÁRTA / 18 MARCH

Fearnóg
Alder

[far-nowg]

Tá foraoisí fearnóg i gCiarraí agus i gCorcaigh.
There are forests of alder in Kerry and Cork.

Alder, the Trailblazer
18 MARCH–14 APRIL

If you were born between now and mid-April, your Celtic tree is the alder – the tree with those tiny little cones on their branches. It's a powerful strong wood. We used it to make shields for protection when we roamed this land on horseback and on foot as tribes. Canal gates and sluices used the alder too, pushing the flow of water along, keeping it moving, getting things done. They're the traits of the alder people, the trailblazers.

19 MÁRTA / 19 MARCH

Ag plé le ...
Involved in ...

[egg play leh]

Bím ag plé le rudaí difriúla.
I'm involved in various things.

Irish people have a great knack of being involved in a lot of different things, so this is a useful phrase for all those people who do charity work: 'I'm involved in an afterschool programme for underprivileged children' or 'I'm in involved in raising money for Alzheimer's research'. But we have an even greater talent for not telling people exactly what we work at.

'What do you do for a living?'

'I'm involved in computers.'

They could be building them, selling them or the Vice-President of Dell – it's so general it could be anything. It's like a farmer saying 'I do a bit of dairy and a bit of tillage', like farming is their hobby instead of their livelihood. *Ag plé le* is a great phrase if you're trying to be vague.

20 MÁRTA / 20 MARCH

Oigheann micreathonnach
Microwave oven

[eye-an mick-ra-hun-uck]

Tá an t-oigheann micreathonnach céanna agam le fiche bliain anuas.
I've had the same microwave for 20 years.

21 MÁRTA / 21 MARCH

Sách fada
Long enough

[sawk fa-da]

Chaith mé deich mbliana san Astráil; bhí me sách fada ann.
I spent 10 years in Australia; I was long enough there.

A lovely Connemara phrase for when you're sitting in the car waiting for your partner to finish at the dentist's. You're an hour and a half in and it was only supposed to be a check-up. You were there sách fada.

22 MÁRTA / 22 MARCH

Sclamhach
Hectoring

[sclav-ack]

Bhí an fear sclamhach leis an bpolaiteoir.
The man was hectoring the politician.

This is a cameo word for the book and I couldn't resist putting it in. To hector someone is to give out or shout at someone. I never knew that you could 'hector' someone or have a 'hectoring' voice. Next time you're at a match, you might hear someone sclamhach *if they're really annoyed with the ref.*

23 MÁRTA / 23 MARCH

Fan socair
Don't move

[fon suck-er]

'Fan socair!' arsa an mháthair leis an bpáiste beag.
'Don't move!' said the mother to the small child.

You can almost hear the authority when you say this phrase: *'Fan socair!'* It's a useful one for teachers to say to a rowdy class or an army sergeant addressing his soldiers.

My introduction to standing really still was in the Gaeltacht at Coláiste na bhFiann. Every morning and evening, we would have a flag ceremony and sing two songs: 'Amhrán na bhFiann' and 'Amhrán an Choláiste'. It was pretty militaristic when I look back on it, but who doesn't want to be in the army when they're 12? It's like watching *Yellowstone* now and wishing you were a cowboy.

I worked my way up the ranks and by the time I was 15 or 16, I was the Parade Commander of over a hundred kids and that meant I got to shout orders at them:

PARÁID! PARÁID AIRE! (Parade! Parade attention!)

SEASAIGÍ AR AIS! (Stand up at ease! [This would be army-style: legs spread, hands behind back, elbows out.])

FANAIGÍ SOCAIR! (Don't move!)

ARDAÍTEAR AN BHRATACH NÁISIÚNTA! (Raise the national flag!)

In the morning time, three lads would go over and raise the Irish flag up the pole, and in the evening they would take it down and do that special flag fold to make it look like a triangle, and the rest of us were so still we were barely blinking. Then that was that for the day and we were off to the céilí.

24 MÁRTA / 24 MARCH

Bolcán
Volcano

[bull-cawn]

Phléasc an bolcán den chéad uair le fiche bliain anuas i mbliana.
The volcano erupted for the first time in 20 years this year.

I picked up this word when I was in Montserrat, travelling through the Caribbean for the TV show. We sailed in from Antigua on a yacht and the island of Montserrat in the distance was spectacular. The huge volcano called the Soufrière Hills reaching into the sky had that look of a remote tropical island that you see in movies. It was like something out of *Jurassic Park*.

We were all brought up with stories about the great volcanoes of the world – Mount Etna, Vesuvius, Krakatoa – but we didn't really think they existed outside of movies until the unpronounceable Eyjafjallajökull in Iceland erupted and all the flights were cancelled.

It was a big deal for Iceland, but it was an even bigger deal for Joe Duffy:

'Joe here on *Liveline*. Who am I speaking to?'

'It's Mary here from Leitrim and my Toyota Starlet is ruined with the ash.'

'Really, Mary? Tell me more.'

'It's like cocaine all over the windscreen, Joe.'

A *bolcán* in Iceland and cocaine on a windscreen in Leitrim. Another classic *Liveline* moment.

25 MÁRTA / 25 MARCH

Míshocair
Uneasy

[mee-huck-er]

Bhí an fear míshocair sa phost nua ar feadh na chéad míosa nó mar sin.
The man was very uneasy in the new job for the first month or so.

When your child isn't settling in crèche, when you get that fidgety nervousness at a meeting when you look across the table at you know who, when your gut tells you something just doesn't feel right ... you are míshocair.

26 MÁRTA / 26 MARCH

Casta
Tricky

[cos-ta]

Tá an bóthar casta agus tú ag tiomáint trína sléibhte.
The road is tricky driving through the mountains.

When your son or daughter is doing the Leaving Cert and you've been up to high doh, lighting so many candles that you're burning the feet off the holy statues, the last thing you want to hear when they come back from an exam and they say it was *casta*. *Casta* is never good news. It's the word that follows honours level English Paper 1 and Maths Paper 1 every year.

An exam can be tricky, a break-up can be tricky, and a person can be tricky – a *duine casta*, those tricky people to get along with. And there are some really, really tricky places to get to in Ireland. That windy and tight road to Castletownbere is grand in the light of day, but it's shite trying to drive it at night. And Mayo? Mayo goes on forever. You can leave Blacksod Bay and drive for two hours to Claremorris – and you're still in fucking Mayo. Mayo is the Canada of Ireland and it's *casta* to navigate.

27 MÁRTA / 27 MARCH

Léacht
Lecture

[lay-okht]

Ní dheachaigh mé chuig mórán do mo chuid léachtaí san ollscoil.
I never went to many of my lectures at university.

I didn't even know I was studying linguistics in college until somebody told me I had an exam in it. About eight months into studying Irish in Trinity, someone comes up to me and says, 'Are you coming down to this linguistics exam?' I didn't know I had linguistics lectures, I didn't know I had a linguistics teacher, and I definitely didn't know I had a linguistics exam. It was complete and utter carnage.

Not going to lectures is part and parcel of the college experience, but I didn't even know this was on my curriculum. There are people who cannot turn up to lectures from one end of the year to the other, but they manage to catch up and do grand in the exam. That wasn't me. I failed first year miserably and was thrown out of college, and I got a big *léacht* about it from my mam, Trina, back in Navan when she found out.

28 MÁRTA / 28 MARCH

Rosc peile
Football chant

[rusk pell-a]

Bhí na roisc pheile le cloisteáil san aer agus muid ag siúl go dtí Old Trafford.
The football chants could be heard in the air as we walked to Old Trafford.

'U.N.I.T.E.D., United are the team for me. With a knick-knack, Paddywhack, give the dog a bone. Why don't Liverpool fuck off home?' An entry-level rosc peile.

29 MÁRTA / 29 MARCH

Strúisín
Stew

[stroo-sheen]

Bíonn blas níos deise ar an strúisín an lá dár gcionn.
A stew tastes better the next day.

30 MÁRTA / 30 MARCH

Poll
Hole

[powl]

Bhí na tumadóirí Red Bull ag tumadh isteach i bPoll na bPéist ar Inis Mór.
The Red Bull divers were diving into Poll na bPéist on Inis Mór.

Whether it's a hole in your trousers, a hole in your wall or a hole in your bucket, *poll* is a great word to have in your Irish vocabulary.

There's an amazing place on Inis Mór called Poll na bPéist – it means 'wormhole' in English. It's a naturally occurring water pool where the rock is cut into a perfect square and the water rushes in from the ocean underneath. They held the Red Bull cliff-diving contest there a few years back and I got to be the MC. It has to be one of the coolest things I've ever done and one of the coolest spots to dive in.

At the bottom, the water is wild and powerful, but at the top of the cliff when you look down at the crashing waves, it really lives up to its name – it's a wormhole made of rock and water.

31 MÁRTA / 31 MARCH

Tranglam tráchta
Traffic jam

[trang-lam trawkht-ah]

Bhí tranglam tráchta dochreidte sa bhaile mór ar maidin.
There was an incredible traffic jam in town this morning.

It only takes one tractor in a country village to cause a traffic jam; they don't just belong to the M50. One bulldozer humming along at 20 kilometres an hour or a load of red-and-white traffic cones making the road narrower can create havoc. You can't drive around Ireland without meeting a tranglam tráchta.

1 AIBREÁN / 1 APRIL

Ceadúnas tiomána
Driver's licence

[kyad-oo-nas tim-awn-a]

Fuair mé mo cheadúnas tiomána inné.
I got my driver's licence yesterday.

We all know getting your passport is pretty important; it's a milestone in your life, like your twenty-first or getting married. But when you get your first ceadúnas tiomána, *it's an epic moment, no matter what age you are. It's a passport to the high roads and the byroads of our country.*

Torbán
Tadpole

[tur-bawn]

Thug na páistí torbáin isteach do bhord an dúlra.
The children brought tadpoles in for the nature table.

3 AIBREÁN / 3 APRIL

Trosc
Cod

[trusk]

Tá an trosc ar cheann de na héisc Éireannaigh den scoth.
Cod is one of the great Irish fish.

I love a bit of fish for dinner, especially on a Friday – which sounds a bit Catholic-Churchy, but it's always been fish-and-chips day in our house. It's funny when you think about it: we are an island nation and we have the richest waters in the world, but we don't seem to value it. It's like we don't want fish stinking up our modern kitchens. We should be eating way more fish, but most of it goes to European markets.

I learned loads about the fishing industry when I went out on a trawler with the O'Flaherty Brothers to film *Hector Goes Fishing*. We were passing an island off the coast of Wexford before heading about 100 miles out to sea, and one of the fishermen says to us, 'This is the last coverage you're going to have for two days and two nights, so call your family and tell them you love them,' and I did.

There's nothing idyllic about the sea in November. It's grey, it's dark, it's cold and it's expansive. I spent three days and three nights on the boat and it was horrific. The smell of tobacco and puke and socks down in the galley was overpowering. I ended up spending most of the three days in the kitchen above the galley, looking out at the horizon, because I couldn't put up with the smell of men and diesel.

I finally managed to eat a bit of stew after two days, when we were on our way back to land. And when I got to the hotel in Kilkenny, the reception desk was rocking and tilting. My feet were on land, but my mind was still at sea.

So fair play to the fishermen who put a lovely bit of *trosc* on our tables for dinner. It's not an easy way to make a living.

4 AIBREÁN / 4 APRIL

Maolcheann
Skinhead

[mwale-kyown]

Bhíodh na maolchinn i gcónaí ag crochadh timpeall ar Shráid Grafton.
The skinheads used to always hang around Grafton Street.

When I was growing up in Navan, there were rockers and punks and New Romantics, but we hadn't any skinheads. I'd only ever see them around Grafton Street in Dublin when I was up. That was the place to be seen. I used to love their vibe: the short jeans with braces, red check shirts, 16-hole oxblood Doc Martens, shaved heads.

Then one day, the skinheads came to Navan. It was back in the day when ska was massive and it was cool as fuck to be into it: Madness, The Beat, The Specials, The Selecter all doing their thing, hit after hit. And somehow an English band called Bad Manners was playing live in my hometown, in the exhibition centre on the Trim Road. Their lead singer was a huge madman called Buster Bloodvessel whose trademark was sticking out his tongue. Their big song at the time was 'Lip Up Fatty'. I still know that tune inside out.

That Saturday in Navan, there were hundreds of ska boys and ska girls all over town, the girls with one little wisp of hair at the front of their heads. The *maolchinn* were in town and I thought it was class.

5 AIBREÁN / 5 APRIL

Sreang
Wire

[shrang]

Go minic feiceann tú péire bróg ag crochadh ar shreang ar an sráid.
You regularly see a pair of shoes hanging over a wire on the street.

———————————

A useful everyday word and also a decent name for a metal band, if you ask me. I can hear the power riffs.

6 AIBREÁN / 6 APRIL

Cnaipe
Switch/button

[knopp-a]

Bhí an cnaipe briste ar an mballa sa halla.
The switch was broken on the wall in the hall.

Cnaipe is a rare word, with the 'n' straight after the 'c'; a unique word for an everyday item. It's onomatopoeic – I can hear the popper on a babygro, the button on the Burco in the local GAA club or the big red switch you press to turn on your oven in the bungalow. Although these days you probably have a brushed-metal German-made dimmer switch.

Buttons are underrated little things. From the button you press to turn on the kettle to the delicate buttons on your shirt on your wedding day, *cnaipí* tell the stories of our lives. It's 11 o'clock and the wedding mass is at 12; you're all ready to go when the button pops off your shirt. Then you have to run around the house looking for the sewing kit you got out of a Christmas cracker and the right colour thread to stitch it back on.

The great Irish mammies of this nation could sew a button back on, and I'd say most men could as well back in the day. Now you would sooner buy a new shirt than try to thread a needle. My mother was a great woman for sewing a button on a shirt. She'd have it back on inside 10 minutes if you were heading out on a Saturday night. *Cnaipí* and the people who can sew them are to be cherished.

7 AIBREÁN / 7 APRIL

Laoch
Legend

[lay-okh]

Tá laochra CLG againn i ngach contae sa tír.
We have GAA legends in every county in the country.

You might know this word from *Laochra Gael* on TG4, a series that celebrates the greatest players of the GAA: the stalwarts of the game, the ones who were different.

We have been making legends for hundreds of years on this island: Cú Chulainn, Queen Medb and Gráinne Mhaol are all *laochra na tíre seo*. We have national *laochra*, local *laochra* and plenty of unsung *laochra* in parishes up and down the country. But sport in particular creates the legends of the land these days, whether it's with the parish club, at the county final or the biggest day of all in Croke Park.

I was in Croke Park in 2024 for the All-Ireland Hurling Final. It was Cork versus Clare, and myself and my eldest boy, Rían, were in the Lower Hogan stand. What 82,300 people witnessed that day was out of this world. It was one of the greatest games of hurling ever played, an epic battle that went into extra time. It was full of skill and drama, twists and turns, ebbs and flows … and then a moment of pure Irish magic from a wizard of a hurler. Tony Kelly from Ballyea in County Clare scored one of the greatest goals ever seen in an All-Ireland Final. I'm sure TG4 have him on the horizon for the *Irish Legends* series when he hangs up his boots and leaves the hurl outside the door. Tony Kelly – *laoch an Chláir agus laoch Gaeil*.

8 AIBREÁN / 8 APRIL

Foirgneamh
Building

[fur-gah-niv]

Tá foirgneamh nua á thógáil in aice na scoile.
There's a new building going up beside the school.

We've been mixing cement in Ireland for generations. We are the great cement mixers, plasterers, roofers and fixers of the world. There's not a big building in a city in England or America that hasn't been constructed by Irish hands.

During Covid, I built a wall between my own and my neighbour's house. I had a big fence there and I loved it. I'd paint it every two years and take care of it, but it was rickety after getting a hammering from storms over the last 15 years. So I had to get a wall and, as the saying goes, a wall makes good neighbours – but I actually think my neighbours are great.

So the building lads came out with a lorry and it was some satisfaction seeing them offload my cinder blocks. Then they got the cement mixer going – *gadunk, gadunk, gadunk.* It looked like it had mixed about 75,000 mixes in its long life. They threw in the cement, sand, rock and customary half a bucket of water. When they got the exact cocktail they were looking for, it was dumped into a wheelbarrow and over to the blocklayer.

I think blocklayers are the great Irish artists of construction, and this man in his late sixties standing in my garden was like Picasso. I felt like I was watching Michelangelo create *David*. I was fascinated watching him work. He probably built many *foirgnimh* in his years. I knew any *foirgneamh* made by those hands would be a good *foirgneamh*.

9 AIBREÁN / 9 APRIL

Cúinne
Corner

[koo-nya]

Shuigh muid sa chúinne agus d'ól muid piontaí Guinness an oíche ar fad.
We sat down in the corner and drank pints of Guinness all night long.

Where's your favourite corner? The corner of the sofa in your sitting room, the comfy seat by the fire, down in the local bar tucked away in the snug? Corners are sanctuaries.

If something is *timpeall an chúinne* (around the corner), it's a good place to be. There's the corner sweet shop, the school around the corner, the corner pub. There's even a pub in Skibbereen called The Corner Bar, and if you go there with your friends you'll still want to find a lovely corner seat in The Corner Bar, because there's something about a 90-degree angle that provides a good vantage point.

Corners are for catching up and having nice chats. You bump into people you know at corners. *Cúinní* are great conversation starters: isosceles triangles of communication.

10 AIBREÁN / 10 APRIL

Deatach
Smoke

[dyah-tukh]

Chonaic mé deatach san aer i bhfad uaim ar an sliabh.
I saw smoke in the air far away on the mountain.

11 AIBREÁN / 11 APRIL

Cáis
Cheese

[kawsh]

An bhfuil aon rud níos deise ná cáis ar arán sóide?
Is there anything nicer than cheese on soda bread?

I was really fond of the Galtee cheese in a box. You don't see cheddar in a box much any more, unless it's overpriced and in a Christmas hamper. This box was made of cardboard with a big red 'GALTEE' on it and a cow looking you directly in the face. It held a big family-sized lump of cheddar. The girl from Calvita became famous because she was on the front of a million boxes of Calvita cheese made every year in the UK. England had Calvita and the little blonde girl, and Ireland had Galtee and two of our finest-looking Friesians.

When I lived in Bilbao, one of the major pluses of me learning Spanish was being able to go into the supermarket and ask for slices of specialised cheese. They had massive round wheels of cheese called Gran Capitán, and they'd cut it right there and then for you at the deli counter. Not a cardboard box in sight.

But in Navan, we stuck with the big blocks of orange Irish cheddar. Nobody in Navan even eats soft cheeses; they're only for posh people in Kildare.

12 AIBREÁN / 12 APRIL

Broim
Fart

[breem]

Cé a lig broim?
Who farted?

When we got to fifth year in school, we got hardback copybooks for projects and essays, and we realised fairly quickly that they provided excellent amplification. If you farted on one, you could hear it up the hallway.

Then we discovered that the smell would stay on the copybook for about a minute after, so the boys would hold you and put the book up to your face, or worse ... they'd give it to you and ask you to hand it up to the teacher.

So in classes like biology, where we used hardback copybooks all the time, or in study periods in the library, there would be a cacophony of farts. We became experts at farting and acoustics.

Everyone has their own unique farting style, except for Irish mothers, whose farts all sound and smell the same. Between six and seven on a Sunday evening was my mother's time to fart. She'd have a sneaky little fart during *Songs of Praise*. My dad always farted in the car and we'd all applaud from the back of the Ford Cortina. And he was a Guinness drinker, so the smell was distinctive.

Some people are weird about *bromanna*, but they're part of life, and if you know someone well, they can be as identifiable as their voice.

13 AIBREÁN / 13 APRIL

Salann agus piobar
Salt and pepper

[sol-in aw-gus pyu-ber]

Is breá liom salann agus piobar i m'anraith.
I love salt and pepper in my soup.

I remember the *salann agus piobar* of the 1980s – the Saxa salt shakers and white pepper that looked more like sand than seasoning. But they became redundant, got left in the back of the press when the Celtic Tiger came around and we got very exotic with our salt and pepper. It was sea salt or pink crystals from the Himalayas, and our pepper came in 'corns'. And with the rock salt and peppercorns came the engineering, because you have to grind them on the go. Big, tall, sleek grinders to crush tiny peppercorns. Some of them even have motors. Fine table salt and white pepper have been relegated to sachets in cafés and B & Bs. You might be lucky enough to encounter an old-school cellar of white pepper at the afters of a funeral in the countryside to put on your soup.

I adore salt and pepper on my boiled egg in the morning and on my tomato and basil soup on a winter's day, I put it on my turnip and mashed potato, with vinegar on my chips – love the stuff. And then there was Salann agus Piobar who were on Top of the Pops in 1988 with their big hit 'Push It'. *Salann agus piobar* – you can't have one without the other.

14 AIBREÁN / 14 APRIL

Greim le hithe
Grab a bite to eat

[grime leh hi-ha]

Stopfaimid sa chéad bhaile eile agus beidh greim againn le hithe.
We'll stop in the next town and grab a bite to eat.

Greim means to grab something – if you slip, you'll grab onto something to stop yourself from falling over. So *greim le hithe* is to grab something quick to eat. It's for your long journeys from Donegal to Wexford. If you've to be at your destination for a certain time and you're on a five-hour trip, you only have a few minutes to stop and grab something to eat. It conjures up an image of standing beside your car at a service station eating a sandwich out of a plastic packet, with the packet of Keogh's crisps and the bottle of water you got in the meal deal. You're back on the road in 10 minutes and on your way to your cousin's wedding.

You can also have *greim le hithe* on a night out. But this isn't for your three-course à la carte in a restaurant – it's a slice of pizza before you head into the gig or the kebab you eat on your walk home. You might be able to push it to dropping in to a tapas place for a glass of wine and some patatas bravas, but that's the extent of it. *Greim le hithe* has to be quick.

15 AIBREÁN / 15 APRIL

Saileach
Willow

[sile-okh]

Bhí an tsaileach ag fás ar bhruach na habhann.
The willow was growing on the bank of the river.

Willow, The Observer
15 APRIL–12 MAY

If you were born around this time of year, the Celtic tree of your birth is the willow. Willows are capable of great empathy and are a source of support for others. What a lovely tree to have as your birth tree – a tree that means so much. The tree is linked to the colour silver. Willows love the rivers and the canals. These Celtic trees are all around us; our ancient tribal forefathers believed the natural world was connected with us and we with these trees' cycle of life.

16 AIBREÁN / 16 APRIL

Maighnéad
Magnet

[my-nayd]

Cheannaigh mé maighnéad i Maidrid le haghaidh an chuisneora sa bhaile.
I bought a magnet in Madrid for the fridge at home.

I used to think fridge magnets were for silly people; now my fridge is covered in them. I've been travelling the world for 22 years, but I've only started collecting them in about the last eight years or so, and now I'm addicted to it.

I've been to all these really amazing places, and once I started picking up fridge magnets as I travelled, I got into a rhythm – Siberia, Ulaanbaatar, Chengdu, Antigua. My favourite is my Rastafari one from Jamaica. My brother Mark in Navan has been collecting them for years and his fridge looks really cool, so when I'm away I pick one up for myself and another one for him. But I will not buy them at the airport – I don't want a heart with 'Welcome to Prague' on it. I buy from local people in the middle of small towns, and the more basic it looks, the better. I usually only get magnets from places I've been to, but Rosco was in India recently filming with the BBC and he texted me, 'Any craic?' I replied, 'No craic. Get me a fridge magnet in India.' It was missing from my collection. I'm sure there are some great fridge magnet collectors reading this who would feel the same.

When I was away in the Aran Islands and in the Basque Country, before fridge magnets, we had postcards. I used to send them to my mother, who would then keep them on top of the TV for about five years. But now the postcard you would get from your auntie on her holidays in Lanzarote isn't a novelty any more, so we've graduated to *maighnéid*.

17 **AIBREÁN** / 17 APRIL

Tinn tuirseach
Sick and tired

[teen tur-shock]

Tá mé tinn tuirseach den phleidhcíocht seo.
I'm sick and tired of this messing.

Our secondary school English class took a trip to Dublin once to do a drama improv for a bunch of students studying Drama in UCD. Away we went and the craic was lively on the bus, as it would be with a load of messers down the back.

We reached Dublin and the driver took the route through the city centre, and there we spotted a woman driving a Mini Cooper behind us. Around O'Connell Street, one of the lads decided to moon out the back window, and so when one did it, we all did. There were seven arses hanging out the back of the bus. It was an extended moon – a full-meat lunar eclipse.

Things escalated quickly and soon enough we saw blue lights flashing and the bus was pulled in. You've never seen so many lads move out of the back seat at pace in your life. We were jumping over seats like gazelles. I think I ended up in row five by the time a garda put his head in the door of the bus and spoke to Richie Ball, our legend of an English teacher.

A week later, the seven of us were hauled in to the principal's office in school. Here was Spud Murphy, a principal who put the fear of God in everyone who crossed his path, so we were nervous – then in walked a garda and the woman who was driving the Mini Cooper. It was a line-up.

We all had to apologise, and Spud Murphy snarled at us, 'I'm sick and tired of ye, the same lads messing all the time. That's it, ye pack of gurriers, ye are suspended!' There wasn't a teacher in that school who wasn't *tinn tuirseach* of the lot of us.

Dochtúir Máirtíní
Doc Martens

[doc-toor mar-teen-ee]

Tá na Dochtúir Máirtíní ar ais i bhfaisean arís.
Doc Martens are all the rage again.

19 AIBREÁN / 19 APRIL

Fínéagar leann úll
Apple cider vinegar

[feen-eh-gar lyan ool]

– Ar mhaith leat aon rud ón ollmharghadh?
– Sea, fínéagar leann úll, le do thoil.
– Do you want anything in the supermarket?
– Yeah, apple cider vinegar, please.

This one is for the health nuts. Apple cider vinegar has been around for hundreds of years and then it dropped off the face of the Earth until Instagram revived it. Now everyone has a bottle, because we all want to revolutionise our gut health.

We're living in a world now where social media tell us what to do. I even have a bottle of apple cider vinegar that came all the way from California, the land of tans and healthy guts. Two teaspoons of *fínéagar leann úll* mixed with a teaspoon of cayenne pepper will change your life. It's become a liquid we can't live without since it appeared on our social media feeds in 2018.

20 AIBREÁN / 20 APRIL

Bearna
Gap

[bar-nah]

Glór an Tube i Londain: 'Seachain an bhearna.'
The sound of the London Tube: 'Mind the gap.'

We've got many great gaps in Ireland: the Gap of Dunloe, the Sally Gap, even Bearna *in County Galway – and don't forget the gap in the hedge, the gap in the wall and the gap in the fence.*

21 AIBREÁN / 21 APRIL

Crios
Belt

[kriss]

Úsáidim an crios céanna gach lá.
I use the same belt every day.

A man needs three things in life: a power washer, a ride-on lawnmower and a decent crios.

22 AIBREÁN / 22 APRIL

Francach
Rat

[frawn-cokh]

Chonaic mé francach ag mo bhosca bruscair.
I saw a rat at my rubbish bin.

If Nidge in Love/Hate *spoke Irish, he'd use this word every day: 'Know what you are? You're a fucking francach.'*

23 AIBREÁN / 23 APRIL

Gaiste luch
Mousetrap

[gash-ta lukh]

Chuir me píosa cáise ar an ngaiste luch.
I put a piece of cheese on the mousetrap.

Growing up in a country bungalow, there were always mice around, and where there are mice there are mousetraps. We'd have traps in the corner of the kitchen, behind the cooker, behind the washing machine, out in the garage. They were big, old-school wooden traps that would take the finger off ya, and we'd use a bit of cheese to tempt the mice, just like in the cartoon *Tom and Jerry*.

Pulling the metal part back to set the trap was dangerous, so it was my father's job to set them. The traps were his domain – he was Tom hunting for all the Jerrys that might have snuck into the kitchen. Thankfully he fared better than the poor cartoon cat.

My father was always proud when there was a mouse caught. He would remove the kill carefully and then fire it over the hedge. And like all good Irish dads, he'd set the trap again and wait ...

24 AIBREÁN / 24 APRIL

Snoíodóir adhmaid
Woodcarver

[snee-o-dor eye-mid]

Tá tallann iontach ag snoíodóirí adhmaid.
Woodcarvers have a wonderful talent.

You never meet a woodcarver who's 90 miles a minute. They go at a slow pace, probably because they work with wood – it's an extension of who they are.

Rollóg earraigh
Spring roll

[rull-owg ar-ee]

Is breá liom rollóga earraigh ó China Garden san Uaimh.
I love spring rolls from China Garden in Navan.

26 AIBREÁN / 26 APRIL

Cálslá
Coleslaw

[kawls-law]

Is náisiún cálslá muid in Éirinn.
We are a coleslaw nation in Ireland.

———————

You can't have a cold-meat salad without coleslaw ... or lasagne ... or a sandwich. There are people in Ireland who take cálslá *on holiday with them.*

27 AIBREÁN / 27 APRIL

Sála arda
High heels

[saw-la or-da]

Níl sé éasca siúl sna sála arda.
It's not easy to walk in high heels.

———————

Who are we trying to fool? Irish women are feet-on-the-ground people. They're not made for high heels – it's why you always see the sála arda *in their hands instead of on their feet at the end of the night.*

28 AIBREÁN / 28 APRIL

Hairicíní
Hurricanes

[har-i-kee-nee]

Bíonn stoirmeacha againn in Éirinn, ach bíonn hairicíní acu i réigiún Mhuir Chairib.
We get storms in Ireland, but the Caribbean gets hurricanes.

I went to a beautiful place called Treasure Beach in Jamaica for the travel show. We stayed in a little 20-bedroom hotel called Jake's, and we'd go to a Rasta shack called Eggy's on the beach to listen to a bit of reggae and have a cold Red Stripe beer. The place was tiny – it was made from corrugated iron and covered in beer signs. We met some great people and had a brilliant time filming. Then, only four weeks after we left, the place was obliterated by a hurricane.

Even though the Caribbean islands are idyllic and spectacularly beautiful, with their white sandy beaches, the danger of living there from one season to another is horrific. We're blessed, geographically speaking, in Ireland. Yes, we get a lot of rain and flooding, but we're lucky we're not in the path of hurricanes. We think we get bad storms here, but we have never felt anything like a *hairicín* rising up through the Gulf of Mexico and blowing carnage across the Caribbean.

29 AIBREÁN / 29 APRIL

Tuilte
Floods

[til-tcha]

Tá na tuilte ag éirí níos measa chuile gheimhreadh sa tír seo.
The floods are getting worse every winter in this country.

We have a bridge over the River Clare in the village near me, and for years it flooded its banks. The water was so fast and high that the single eye of the bridge couldn't handle it, so it rose over the bridge and up the banks. One time the village was flooded for a week, and the detour to get to Galway city by car took 25 minutes. It was impassable, so if you wanted to get in and out of the village to do business, there was a local man who would give you a lift across the river in his boat.

During that same flood, RTÉ *Prime Time* did a broadcast from Claregalway; Miriam O'Callaghan went live from the bridge. She had to go to the home of Teresa Mannion, even if it meant making an unnecessary journey. We were home watching the TV and there down the road was Miriam with her microphone in her hand, and the local man rowing across the river with his passengers.

The bridge has since been widened, the water now flows through new eyes and the floods have abated. However, all over the land, nothing much has been done to help the villages and towns that flood every year. We need to adapt to the changes in the climate. We can't all have a local man row us across the river to get our litre of milk.

30 AIBREÁN / 30 APRIL

Mála spíosraí
Spice bag

[maw-la spees-ree]

D'ordaigh me mála spíosraí aréir sa siopa sceallóg áitúil.
I ordered a spice bag last night in the local chipper.

The spice bag craze has boomed over the last 10 years or so. You can even buy 'spice bag mix' in supermarkets now and put it on your chips at home, but I feel like spice bags aren't as big a thing in the West. My young lads like them, and I'd have one the odd time, but I've already made public my love of a good snack box. A base of proper Italian chipper chips with two decent pieces of chicken on top, and one has to be a breast.

The only 'spice' we had in the great chippers in Navan in my day was a spice burger. We never even knew what was in it; it was just 90 per cent mystery and 10 per cent beautiful. It was either that or a battered sausage, which we all called a 'widow's memory'. We used to go into the chipper and shout, 'Two large cod and chips and three widow's memories, please' and they knew exactly what we meant. We were a long way from *málaí spíosraí*.

1 BEALTAINE / 1 MAY

Piseog
Superstition

[pish-owg]

Tá Éire lán de phiseoga.
Ireland is full of superstitions.

If you go back to any major town in the 1960s, someone knew someone who had 'the cure' for something. I used to have nosebleeds at night-time when I was a kid. It happened a couple of times a month until one day my dad said, 'Right, we're sorting this out.' We drove across to Trim to a holy woman's house, where she said a prayer, rubbed my nose, lit a candle and gave me a coin. She said, 'When your nose stops bleeding, light a candle for me.'

My brother Freddie got the same treatment for his warts. My dad drove us to a pub called The Silver Tankard on the Kells-to-Navan Road, where we met a lad who had the cure for warts. He rubbed my brother's hand, lit a candle and gave him a coin while my dad went and had a pint.

And it worked. The nosebleeds and the warts stopped. But is it a *piseog*? I don't know and it doesn't matter, because I love superstitions. Being brought to a healer was a sign of the times: that we all knew people in different parishes and we shared stories, we shared knowledge and we minded each other.

But what do we believe, anyway? That everything you buy in a pharmacy will cure you? You can go to Eastdoc or Westdoc or a 24-hour mobile clinic for your warts, but back in the 1960s in Meath, you went to a man in a pub with a candle. I think we still need *piseoga* to make us feel like something else is happening outside of us and our mobile phones.

Crosóg mhara
Starfish

[cruss-owg waa-ra]

Tá crosóga mara ar fud na tránna sa tír seo.
There are starfish all over the beaches in this country.

3 BEALTAINE / 3 MAY

Thar a bheith
Extremely

[har a veh]

Tá mé thar a bheith sásta le mo thorthaí ón Ardteist.
I'm extremely happy with my Leaving Cert results.

Thar a bheith is an adverb you can use when you have strong feelings about something. You were extremely happy with your results from college or someone was extremely insulting at the meeting. It can be a positive or a negative thing, but you wouldn't use it for feeling hungry – that's *an*: *an-ocras* (serious hunger).

We love using the word 'extreme', even in English. When there's a cold snap or a storm coming, we're all glued to our TVs to see how extreme the weather will be: *Tá sé thar a bheith sleamhain amuigh ansin* (It's extremely slippy out there).

This is a 'break glass in an emergency' word. It's only for the extreme situations:

» Leaving Cert
» Driving test
» Bad weather
» Good weather
» When you've done something to upset your mother.

If you use *thar a bheith*, you have everyone's attention.

Culaith Chomaoineach
Communion suit

[kull-a khom-wee-nokh]

Tá an Chomaoineach ar an mbealach. Caithfimid culaith a cheannach.
The Communion is on the way. We'll have to buy a suit.

My father ran the drapery shop Keogan & Carthy at the top of Trimgate Street, across from St Mary's Church in Navan. It had all the top fashion and it did a great run on Communion suits. It's where I got my First Holy Communion suit. I wore a little bottle-blue suit, with my red locks swept across my head like Steve Davis, a gap in my front teeth and a massive rosette on my jacket like a horse gets at a pony show. I looked like I'd won a gymkhana. It was quality Navan.

We all got into a big family photo, and I still have it to this day. Those kinds of photographs meant so much at the time. They were framed and put in a place of prestige in the house. I'm sure there are many Communion photos from the 1970s and '80s still gracing the good front rooms in houses across the country. Now all of our photos are on our phones, and you might flick back for a look, but it's not the same. Only glossy photos in a wooden frame can truly capture the beauty of a *culaith Chomaoineach*.

5 BEALTAINE / 5 MAY

Faigh réidh le
Get rid of

[fai ray le]

Faigh réidh leis an bhfobhríste dornálaí sin anois!
Get rid of them boxers now!

Faigh réidh le is for that moment when you just have to say it's time to get rid of this – that old jacket, that old bicycle, that old pair of jocks you've had for years and years and another year. It's done.

Boxers have been a real ladder of life for me, from the early days as a teenager getting a cool three-pack from Penneys to moving up in life to a pair of Calvin Klein or Hugo Boss boxers. I was very attached to a few pairs of boxers that lived with me for a long time, through my Basque Country years in Bilbao to my dole and FÁS scheme years in Galway, until one morning when me and my missus were getting ready for a wedding.

I took my favourite pair of jocks from the bottom drawer, and when I attempted to put my foot in, there was a hole big enough in the gusset that I didn't know where my leg should go. They were like a spider's web, hanging on by a thread. So my missus said it was time to *faigh réidh leis an bhfobhríste dornálaí*, and into the bin they went. A great pair of jocks that served me well and supported me (in many ways) over the years.

6 BEALTAINE / 6 MAY

Neart
Plenty, Enough of

[nyart]

Maith go leor, sin é. Tá neart cloiste agam faoi seo.
Right, that's it. I've heard enough of this.

This is one for when you've moved out of home and your mother rings you and is worried about you: 'Have you enough paracetamol? Have you enough blankets? Have you enough bread?'

7 BEALTAINE / 7 MAY

Ag teastáil
Wanting/needing

[egg tas-tall]

An bhfuil níos mó prátaí ag teastáil uait?
Do you want more potatoes?

It was in the kitchen with the *bean an tí* in Ráth Chairn that I first heard *ag teastáil*, and I can tell you, I learned it fairly quick. It was one of the basic conversational building blocks for everyday survival in the Gaeltacht.

You're back in the house for lunch after a busy morning in the *halla* and you're at the table with 15 other young lads. It's Friday afternoon and the *bean an tí* has made chips. She comes in with the tray and asks, '*An bhfuil níos mó sceallóg ag teastáil uaibh?*' She already knows the answer from all 16 of us will be '*Tá*', but what she's trying to do is get that Irish out of us.

Your *bean an tí* is the best teacher in the Gaeltacht. There should be an honours degree in being a *bean an tí*; there should be a union! She is the number one most important person, because she becomes your new mammy for three weeks. We need to appreciate them and mind them. There has been a long succession of *mná tí* in the Gaeltacht, but do we have enough for the future? Summers in the Gaeltacht are part of our DNA as a nation, and we can't have that without *mná tí*. No water, no whiskey, no *mná tí*, no Gaeltacht.

8 BEALTAINE / 8 MAY

Deannach
Dust

[ja-noch]

Tá an deannach go dona faoin leaba.
The dust is awful under the bed.

I'm a bit obsessive about dust. I have three different hoovers around the house, all in strategic locations. I have one in the corner of the kitchen for the dog's hairs, but I *really* like getting under the beds, because the dust under there can be like those Wild West tumbleweeds rolling past a saloon. It takes them weeks and weeks to build, so you have to have a hoover that will get all the way under the bed.

So I have a special hoover that's like an old sort of Electrolux. It's small and it's old school, but it's a powerful little yoke. It means I can get under the bed and exterminate all the dust. I will get down on my hands and knees and *really* get stuck into the pile in the carpet. I even hate the idea of going to sleep if there's dust under the bed. I'm a dust hunter. I could be halfway up the stairs, giving it socks with the hoover, and my boys will just step over me. They won't even say hello, because they know I'm hunting *deannach*.

9 BEALTAINE / 9 MAY

Bungaló
Bungalow

[bung-alow]

Is breá linn bungaló deas in Éirinn.
We love a good bungalow in Ireland.

We called our house 'the bungalow'. I don't know why we started calling it that, but then even the postman knew it as 'the bungalow'. Some people's houses are called 'Ivy Lodge' or 'The Priory', but our house wasn't fancy, so we just called it 'the bungalow'. We lived two miles outside of town and there were no other houses around us, so this was the ingenious plan we came up with before postcodes. Our address was: The Bungalow, Knockumber, Navan, County Meath. Where else would you get away with that?

There are people living in bungalows that still haven't been finished and they started building them in 1974. Some of them are only half-plastered. The pinnacle of affordable housing in Ireland was choosing the plans for your bungalow from the book *Bungalow Bliss*. They were the worst-insulated, worst-designed houses in the world, but you could build them fast and you could build them cheap. Almost as important as whether your door had an alcove was what you put on top of the pillars on either side of the entrance to your driveway. Would you choose the swans or go all Art Deco with the big balls? We went very *Grand Designs* and had a sliding patio door. It was always full of condensation and we could never see out of it, but we thought it was posh.

So many of us were born and reared in the great bungalows of Ireland. We love them so much that we didn't even go too far to come up with the name *as Gaeilge*: *bungaló*.

Dornálaíocht
Boxing

[dur-naw-lee-okt]

Is breá linn féachaint ar dhornálaíocht oíche Dé Sathairn.
We love watching boxing on a Saturday night.

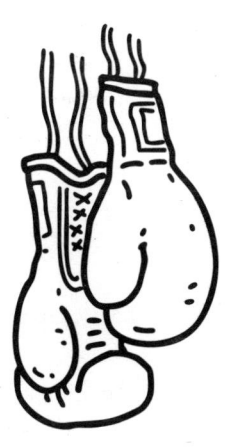

11 BEALTAINE / 11 MAY

Níor mhair sé i bhfad
It didn't last long

[neer var shay i vad]

Níor mhair na Gealáin Thuaidh ach cúpla nóiméad, ach bhí siad togha.
The Northern Lights didn't last long, but they were awesome.

In recent years, the Northern Lights have made an appearance in Ireland, but níor mhair siad i bhfad *(they didn't last long). Even so, the image is entered into the 'WOW!' part of our brains ... and the photo galleries on our phones.*

Tóirse
Torch

[tor-sha]

D'imigh an leictreachas, ach bhí mo thóirse in aice na leapa.
The electricity went, but my torch was beside the bed.

I'm mad into torches. I have one of those big red torches with the handle on top. These massive Eveready torches are a favourite of farmers and search parties, but I think every house should have one. They're what you want for when the dog starts barking at three o'clock in the morning and you have to investigate. The battery is like a cement block – it's around six kilos – so you have to have your spares. A big shout-out to the six-volt carbon zinc battery. Only specific places stock them, but luckily I have a friend who drives the length and breadth of the country to supply shops with torches and batteries, so I have an in.

When I was in Chongqing in China, I had an opportunity to add to my torch collection. This city has about 32 million people in it and it's a manufacturing hub of China. Your phone was built there, parts of your car were built there and they specialise in electronics, so I bought what can only be described as a weapon of a torch. It has 16 different settings and it's probably the most powerful torch in the world. I leave it beside my bed in case the bombs start dropping and the world ends in the middle of the night. You can put your candles away; everyone should have *tóirsí* in strategic positions around the house in case of emergency.

13 BEALTAINE / 13 MAY

Sceach gheal
Hawthorn

[shkyak gyal]

Tá an sceach gheal an-chumhachtach i miotaseolaíocht na hÉireann.
The hawthorn tree is very powerful in Irish mythology.

Hawthorn, the Illusionist
13 MAY–9 JUNE

If you were born at this time of year, the hawthorn is your Celtic tree of birth. It is probably the most powerful of all the great trees we have on the island. Its powers lie deep in its roots, bark and its summering flowers. To be born under the hawthorn is a powerful thing; you have depth and mystery, like the tree itself.

It's revered and celebrated in our folklore. Our ancestors honoured it and worshipped it. It was in every field, every laneway, every boreen, and the word was (and still is) that you don't mess with the hawthorn bush – you leave it alone.

The lads who built the Limerick-to-Ennis bypass know all about the power of the hawthorn. A massive, multimillion-euro dual carriageway construction ground to a halt as the diggers and excavators attempted to remove a hawthorn bush near the Clare Inn that has been there for centuries. The locals knew all about its powers and its curses, and they were determined that it was not going to be touched. So the motorway was built around it, and it's still there to be seen, and always will be.

14 BEALTAINE / 14 MAY

Gloine fíona
A glass of wine

[glin-na fee-un-a]

– An bhfuil gloine fíona ag teastáil uait?
– Tá, an bhfuil Santa Rita agat?
– Would you like a glass of wine?
– Yeah, do you have a Santa Rita?

Forget your Châteauneuf-du-Pape – we couldn't get enough of Santa Rita during the boom years. It was the wine of the Celtic Tiger; there was a ship on loop each month from Chile to Ireland that was full to the brim of Santa Rita. The people of Ireland were knocking it back left, right and centre.

So when I was filming outside Santiago in Chile for the travel show, I wanted to pay homage. We were invited to the winery – one of the oldest vineyards in Chile – by the Santa Rita family themselves.

After the tour outside, we retired to the cellars for a tasting where I met the daughter of the Santa Rita family, the heir to the throne. She thanked me extensively for Ireland's great consumption of her family's wine. Our small country had changed the fortunes of their business, so she wanted to impress us. She took down a 76-year-old bottle of Santa Rita, a deep, dark cab sav, one of those bottles you blow the dust off, and she opened it to celebrate our visit. She was giving it socks, telling us it was one of the great grapes of South America, talking about the tannins and notes of chocolate. I am no connoisseur of wine, but Rosco was filming me, so I went along with it all the same. Then she takes a delicate sip of the wine, and I knew I had to do it … I held the glass up, said 'Cheers', and knocked the whole thing back in one go. She was horrified, but you can't beat a *gloine fíona* of Santa Rita.

15 BEALTAINE / 15 MAY

Portach
Bog

[pur-tokh]

Caithfaimid aire a thabairt do na portaigh sa tír seo.
We need to mind the bogs of our country.

Turf is a legendary natural resource that we have here in Ireland. It grows in a magical ecosystem, a place people know of but not all have been to: the *portach*. It's like an Irish version of Narnia, where fluorescent insects, multicoloured birds and otherworldly flowers flourish. But when your father tells you you're going out to the bog with him tomorrow to help, it's like fucking penance.

Spending a day on the bog is the hardest type of physical labour we have. And the bog doesn't start at 11, it starts at 6 a.m. Then you spend eight to ten hours in the searing sunshine, footing the turf, the bog stretching on and on in the distance. There are no parasols on the bog, nowhere you can shelter or rest. It's relentless. It's a socially acceptable form of child labour in Ireland that starts at the age of six. Anyone who spent their childhood summers helping their father on the bog will remember – that kind of physical labour leaves an indent in the brain.

You can use *portach* for the bog and *portach* for the toilet, but there are no *portaigh* on the *portach* either. Just sunburn and misery.

16 BEALTAINE / 16 MAY

Gual
Coal

[goo-al]

Dhóigh muid gual san Uaimh nuair a bhí mé óg.
We burned coal in Navan when I was young.

Thanks be to God that my family didn't have access to a local bog, and you'll know why from yesterday's word, *portach*. When I was growing up, we were coal and briquettes people – and, of course, slack. Oh yes, the slack of the damp midlands bungalows. It was a concoction of crushed coal moistened with water. My father would mix the dusty, gravel-like bits of coal with water in the grey basin that was always outside our back door. Then, when the coal would be hopping with red heat, he would bring in the slack. He would carefully layer the black, wet, cement-like mixture in a little ridge on the fire, higher and higher, and pat it down nice and tight. After about 15 minutes, the fire would be as hot as a furnace in an industrial steel factory in Sheffield. We would be opening doors and windows in the middle of winter to let the heat out. And it lasted for hours; Dad's job was done.

The coal we used to get sometimes was called Texan coal. What a name for coal – everyone went mad for it for a while. But we mostly used Polish coal. I went to the biggest coal-producing area in Poland for the travel show to pay homage to John Paul II, who was born there, and to give thanks to the coal producers for keeping us warm for years. But there was nothing like a bit of slack on top of the *gual* to get the fire nice and hot. I doubt it's legal now, but at the time it was cheap and it kept us warm. Now if we only knew how to bleed the radiators in the cold bedrooms …

17 BEALTAINE / 17 MAY

Ponc
Dot

[punk]

– *Cén ríomhphost atá agat?*
– *Hector a dó ag Éirinn ponc com.*
– What's your email?
– Hector2@ireland.com.

When the internet came to Ireland and I realised you could get an email address that was '@ireland.com', I was on it like a rash. My first email address was the coolest one I will ever have: Hector1@ireland.com. When work was getting busier and the requests were coming in by email, I thought it was a really cool address to have. But then I lost the password and I couldn't get into my account. I had it for about 10 years, so I was devastated, but retrieving a password 20 years ago was shit hard. So then I changed my email address to the second-best one I will ever have: Hector2@ireland.com.

We would be in the business centre of a hotel in Bangkok or Bolivia and you'd be mad to see what was going on at home, so you'd use the hotel computer to log on to ireland.com and check the news. The landing page had everything you needed to know. They were the innocent days of email and the internet. Now I'm drowning in passwords, and I still miss my original email address. Nothing will ever beat it.

Ponc is one of those words that shows the flexibility of the Irish language. It has adapted to modern usage, and you will hear *ponc* all the time when people are giving out their email addresses, or when they give you the frequency on an Irish-language radio station: Raidió na Life, *céad is a sé ponc a ceathair* FM (106.4 FM).

18 BEALTAINE / 18 MAY

Fabht
Glitch

[fowt]

Bhí fabht san X-Bhosca, bhí an Wi-Fi an-mhall.
The Xbox was glitchy, the Wi-Fi was very slow.

Looking for Wi-Fi in the countryside in the West of Ireland back in the early 2000s was tricky enough. Trying to watch my beloved Man Utd on Sky Sports meant a trip of a few miles to the local pub. Then the kids came along, and took control of the TV with their video games console. For years, all I heard was, 'Dad, what's the story with the Wi-Fi? I'm playing FIFA here and it's glitchy.' It was 'glitchy' this and 'glitchy' that, until one day the future arrived to the parish: fibre broadband.

But it was still about two years before we managed to get a good connection in our house, because every time they tried to run the cable the hundred yards through a pipe under the garden to our kitchen, it would get blocked.

It was Mayo men who were there to install it. Mayo men built New York City and tramlines and subway tunnels, and now they were in our garden trying to install broadband. There were about six of them trying to force a wire through the pipe; one lad's knuckles were even bleeding. But it kept getting stuck. Eventually, they said they might have to dig up the garden. 'You what?' I said. Then another Mayo man came over: 'Okay, okay, we'll try one last thing. Have you got a bit of Fairy Liquid?'

I ran in to get my aquamarine Fairy Liquid and they covered the wire and the pipe with it, then hooshed a bucket of warm water down after it. And we hear the voice of another Mayo lad from the kitchen: 'We got it!' It was like striking oil. We had 5G within 10 minutes, and my oldest lad said, 'This is the best day of my life.' No more *fabhtanna*.

Tua
Hatchet

[too-ah]

Cá bhfuil an tua? Tá mé chun adhmad a ghearradh.
Where's the hatchet? I'm going to chop some wood.

Ruathar
Raid

[roo-eh-hur]

Rinneadh ruathar in Footlocker le linn na gcíréibeacha i mBaile Átha Cliath.
There was a raid in Footlocker during the riots in Dublin.

Raids have evolved from the time of Celtic warriors robbing grain from local tribes to lads raiding toilet paper from supermarkets during the pandemic.

21 BEALTAINE / 21 MAY

Siabhrán
Hallucination

[sheev-rawn]

Bhí mé chomh tinn sin go raibh siabhrán orm sa leaba.
I was so ill, I was hallucinating in the bed.

I remember the time when Ireland went on a mad moving-statue hunt. It started in the small village of Ballinspittle in Cork, where a few locals swore they'd seen a holy statue move. 'I swear to God, I was just sitting there and the Virgin Mary waved at me.' It was the summer of 1985, and within days, thousands had flocked to the site to witness the incredible event.

Then statues started moving all over the country. RTÉ couldn't keep up with the daily miracles. Statues were crying, twitching, glancing – it was like the whole country was on magic mushrooms.

We love a good holy miracle. There's not a mother or grandmother in Navan who hasn't been to Lourdes. There were three or four trips there every year from the parish of St Mary's. The moving statue of Ballinspittle put us on the map with the big money-spinners of Lourdes and Medjugorje until the statue was smashed to pieces. But the question remains: was it real? Or was it a *siabhrán*?

22 BEALTAINE / 22 MAY

Aibí
Ripe

[ab-by]

Is aoibheann liom cáis aibí ar arán donn baile.
I love some mature cheese on homemade brown bread.

You can use aibí *for a ripe avocado or mature cheese. It can also be used to describe a person who's mature but, for me, this is a word for the kitchen.*

23 BEALTAINE / 23 MAY

Ag clamhsán
Grumbling/giving out

[egg klaus-awn]

Níor stop an déagóir ach ag clamhsán an bealach ar fad síos go Corcaigh sa charr.
The teenager never stopped giving out all the way down to Cork in the car.

This is for the parents of the 12- or 13-year-old in the back of the car on a four-hour journey and they won't stop grumbling. It's the age of never being satisfied. 'Stop an clamhsán, will you?'

24 BEALTAINE / 24 MAY

Comharsa bhéal dorais
Next-door neighbour

[kor-sah vale dur-ish]

Bíonn comharsana béal dorais maithe ag teastáil i gcónaí.
Good next-door neighbours are always needed.

The person you ring first when your electricity is gone to see if theirs is gone too. The person who will mind the kids if you're home late. The person you can lean on.

25 BEALTAINE / 25 MAY

Casúr
Hammer

[kas-oor]

'*Cá bhfuil mo chasúr?' arsa an siúinéir.*
'Where's my hammer?' says the carpenter.

Everyone has a hammer and everyone has a Phillips screwdriver, but the most important thing to have is a friend who knows much more than those two tools – your go-to person who can fix everything. That friend, for me, is Clive.

26 BEALTAINE / 26 MAY

Ceibeab
Kebab

[kebab]

Bhíodh ceibeab iontach tigh Ismael in aice leis an Baggot Inn ar feadh na mblianta.
There was a great kebab at Ismael's beside the Baggott Inn for years.

I spent a good few years living in Dublin after I failed first year in university and dropped out. Back then, there was plenty of accommodation and rent was reasonable, and we were only an hour away from home, so we could go back to Navan at the weekend. It was a glorious time to be in the city: the rock 'n' roll scene was buzzing, *The Commitments* movie was out, and we loved nothing more than getting a few gigs in a week. We'd go to The SFX, McGonagle's, The Olympic Ballroom, The Stadium, The Top Hat in Dún Laoghaire, The Rock Garden – it was a treasure trove of venues that hosted the best bands from over the water. Me and my brother Freddie were in our element.

The Baggot Inn was one of the smaller venues where the best young bands of all levels played, and right outside it was Ismael's Kebab House. The place came alive after midnight. You would walk in and see this massive lump of meat that had probably been cooking since about five o'clock. We'd dig into the chicken shawarma with the fresh lettuce and soft pitta bread and special sauce. They were fresh and tasty, and they gave us the soakage we needed after the feed of cans and pints. To us, Ismael's was the best *ceibeab* place in town.

27 BEALTAINE / 27 MAY

Ag éirí as
Giving up/retiring

[eg eye-ree ahs]

Tá Pól ag éirí as tar éis fiche a seacht bliana leis an gcomhlacht.
Paul is retiring after 27 years with the company.

Back in the 1970s, my hometown was one of the biggest carpet-producing areas in Ireland. There wasn't a hallway or sitting room in the country that wasn't covered in carpets made in the factory in Kells. The classic Axminster and Westminster designs provided comfort for the feet of patrons as they walked from their bedrooms out through the corridors of hotels on their way to their continental breakfasts. Navan produced the Rolls-Royce of carpets; they supplied mansions and government buildings, and even got a contract for a casino in Las Vegas in the 1980s. It was such big news that it made the front of the *Meath Chronicle*.

My uncle Micheál worked all his life in the carpet factory in Navan town, and he called in to see us every week for 30 years or more. He would walk in of a Saturday and go, 'How are you? All sitting, I see.' And we would all peel our eyes away from *Blind Date* to say hello, a Navan carpet under our feet that was made down the road in his factory.

Navan carpets were part of Micheál's identity, so when he said he was *ag éirí as* the carpet business, that he was retiring, it was big news in our house. Not long after he retired, the carpet business gave up Navan as well. Everyone had someone in their family who worked in the carpet factory, so when it closed down, it was a massive blow to the town.

But when the carpets left, they were replaced by furniture: now everyone buys their dining tables from Navan. It is a hub of creativity: we gave the world Pierce Brosnan, Tommy Tiernan, Dylan Moran and quality carpets and furniture.

Alt
Knuckle

[awlt]

Scríob mé m'alt ar an mballa.
I scraped my knuckle on the wall.

29 BEALTAINE / 29 MAY

Feabhas
Improvement

[fyows]

Tháinig feabhas ar a chuid Gaeilge théis trí seachtaine sa Ghaeltacht.
His Irish got better after three weeks in the Gaeltacht.

We can use this word in so many great ways, because we love when something improves: the school exam marks, the weather on holidays, the local soccer team and, most importantly, our Irish. To be ag dul i bhfeabhas *is a great goal when learning any language. But this isn't to be used when someone improves after being ill; that's* biseach.

30 BEALTAINE / 30 MAY

Spriocdháta
Deadline

[spruk-gaw-ta]

Ba é an spriocdháta le haghaidh an phoist an 30ú Bealtaine.
The deadline for the job was 30 May.

This is a nice word for the end of the month; that's when deadlines normally fall. I've never had to meet deadlines with my work ... until I wrote a book! But a little bit of pressure pushes us on, doesn't it? So keep an ceann síos (*the head down*) *and hit those* spriocdhátaí!

31 BEALTAINE / 31 MAY

Mionbhóthar
Minor road

[myun-vow-hur]

Chuaigh mé amú ar mhionbhóthar i Maigh Eo.
I got lost on a minor road in Mayo.

We love a road classification so we know where we're driving. There are main roads and minor roads, primary, secondary and tertiary roads. But we still use mionbhóthar *to describe any road outside of Dublin.*

1 MEITHEAMH / 1 JUNE

Scrúdú; Ardteist
Exam; Leaving Cert

[skrew-doo]; [awrd-tesht]

Bhí an aimsir go hálainn agus an scrúdú ar siúl sa scoil.
The weather was lovely while the exam was going on in the school.

I remember the year of my Leaving Cert well, because it was around the time of Maradona's Hand of God at the World Cup. The minute the games were over, we were out playing soccer, so when the Ardteist rolled around I hadn't spent much time studying. But there were ways of cogging back then.

There were about 98 students and one invigilator in the massive gymnasium in our school, so there was no chance we would be caught cheating. The invigilator would sit at the top of the room eating his big packet of Wine Gums and he had no idea how smart we were – not smart enough to actually do the test, but smart enough to cheat.

We had a system where the brainy guy who had all the answers would go, 'Excuse me, can I go to the toilet?' after he'd seen the questions on the exam paper. We knew he was our go-to man, so about 30 seconds later someone else would ask to go to the toilet and we would all steadily go in and get the answers off him. We'd do this for a few subjects, but especially for Latin. And it was all prearranged with the Latin genius in the class.

I ended up getting five Cs in honours papers in the Leaving Cert and, as luck would have it, I did well in Latin. And because of that, I was allowed go to Trinity College – the poshest of posh universities in Ireland – even though I got an E in pass Maths.

2 MEITHEAMH / 2 JUNE

Coicís
Fortnight

[kai-keesh]

Táimid ag dul go Lanzarote go ceann coicíse.
We're going to Lanzarote for a fortnight.

I love the sound of this word *as Gaeilge*, and luckily it's a word we use often in our daily lives. How many times have we said it over a cup of tea? 'When will you be back?' 'In a fortnight.'

When Irish people say 'fortnight', it definitely means holidays. Two weeks is a magical thing. A week or even 10 days isn't long enough – you have to take the fortnight to really get the benefit. You go to places like Puerto del Carmen for a fortnight; Lanzarote is practically the 33rd county at this stage.

We spent a fortnight in Playa Blanca on the far side of Puerto del Carmen a few years ago and we had to go to an Irish pub in the 28-degree heat to see Clare play Limerick in the All-Ireland hurling semi-final. We ambled in in our shorts and flip-flops, and I swear to God, it was like being on the main streets of Limerick. We were all there for our *coicís* in the sun.

3 MEITHEAMH / 3 JUNE

Laghairt
Lizard

[ly-urt]

Rith an laghairt go sciobtha suas an balla.
The lizard ran quickly up the wall.

4 MEITHEAMH / 4 JUNE

Foiche
Wasp

[fwi-hya]

Tháinig an fhoiche isteach trí fhuinneog na cistine.
The wasp came in the kitchen window.

Foiche is another new word for me, but at this time of year I'll be using it a lot, because wasps are out ruining picnics all across the country. They're everywhere.

There were plenty of them around the count in the RDS during the 2024 election. Candidates were swatting them away left, right and centre, and then there was Gerry 'The Monk' Hutch telling journalist Paul Reynolds, 'You're like a dying wasp, you are' for asking him how he felt about losing the election. He probably wanted to squash him.

There are only two ways to get rid of a wasp: one is to open the windows and hope it flies out by itself; the other is to roll up a tea towel really tight and give it a good crack of that when it lands on the kitchen window.

But I think getting stung by a wasp is a rite of passage. Communions and Confirmations and wasp stings are the milestones of childhood. I remember getting wasp stings when I was a kid, but I don't recall my boys ever coming in saying they'd been stung by a wasp. As our days get more structured, the wasps become more gentrified, so maybe they're looking to get their stings in elsewhere – they're probably all off on a *coicís* (fortnight, p. 151) in Lanzarote.

5 MEITHEAMH / 5 JUNE

Boilgeog
Bubble

[bull-gyowg]

Tá iománaí cáilúil i dTiobraid Árann darb ainm Boilgeog Ó Duibhir.
There's a famous hurler in Tipperary called Bubbles O'Dwyer.

When I was in school, we started making bubbles with our mouths. The aim was to create a bubble with your saliva and blow it off your tongue. There was a guy called Damien Mongey and he was the king of it. We thought he was like Uri Geller bending spoons. 'How're you doing that? How're you doing that?' we all started. And then there were about 30 of us sitting in class trying to blow bubbles off our tongues.

It took me weeks, but then I got it: I formed a bubble, blew it out of my mouth, and watched it fly off through the air. Then I'd do another and another. If I got into a good sequence and the viscosity of saliva was right, I could even morph them together and fire off a double or a triple.

Thanks to the complete and utter boredom of Economics or whatever class we were in, I'm now a master *boilgeog*-maker. I've carried the skill with me and I can still fly them off when conditions are right. It's my party piece.

6 MEITHEAMH / 6 JUNE

Scairdscí
Jet ski

[skard-shkee]

Thug mé scairdscí amach ar cíos ar mo laethanta saoire.
I rented out a jet ski on my holidays.

Anyone who thinks it's cool to jet-ski in a lake in Westmeath or in Dún Laoghaire Harbour is fooling themselves. They're the scourge of the waters. The only people who should have scairdscíonna *are big-wave surfers being towed far out to sea off the coast of the Cliffs of Moher.*

7 MEITHEAMH / 7 JUNE

Steall
A splash

[shtall]

Rinne an páiste steall sa linn snámha.
The child made a splash in the swimming pool.

You'll find *steall* in the phrase *ag stealladh báistí*, which means 'lashing rain', so it's all about splashing water here. It makes me think of a child bombing into a swimming pool on their holidays, or a little kid in their brand-new wellies splashing in puddles. I'm not afraid to admit that I still like putting on my wellies and going outside. I have a pair of Hunter wellingtons and they're the BMWs of welly boots, because I've had them for 23 years and I still like splashing outside in them.

Wellingtons are a necessity if you're going to a point-to-point. I brought my two boys to their first point-to-point last year and they wore sparkling-clean Nike runners. At the end of the day, my car had to be towed out of a field, so you can imagine what the runners looked like. They were blocks of muck; you couldn't even tell what they looked like before. There was no way I was having them in the car, so they were left on a wall beside the field. I took a photo of the muck runners on the wall and I said, 'There's no way I'm bringing you to a point-to-point again unless you have a pair of wellingtons.' This year, the two lads had their wellies and were happy out walking through the mud and puddles at the point-to-point.

Children in bright yellow wellies and massive puddles are made for each other. Then, as the years go on, we start saying, 'Don't go in that puddle' and knock ourselves out of it. But we should try not to lose it. When you put on wellingtons, you should always have a smile on your face, because you know you're in for a good *steall*.

8 MEITHEAMH / 8 JUNE

Drithle
Spark

[drih-tleh]

Bhí drithlí ag teacht ón adhmad ar an tine.
There were sparks coming from the wood on the fire.

I love lighting fires. I have a firepit out the back and I look forward to having people around so I can light it, maybe burn a bit of wood. In my dreams I'm always lighting fires, trying to get that spark to get it going. It must be the caveman in me.

I come from a *gual* (coal, p. 137) background, so when my wife said we needed to start burning blocks, I was dead against it – but now it's wood that floats my boat. Whether it's a dry bit of ash, beech or oak, there's nothing better than that spark and the flame and the smell of a log fire in a West of Ireland winter.

I'm an expert at finding a nice bit of wood, as well – I have different suppliers who I call every winter to source logs for the fire. There's a young lad called Daragh who imports wood from the Baltic States and when he says, 'Hector, I have a lovely bit of Baltic ash for you,' I can't wait to get my hands on it. The satisfaction of seeing those Baltic sparks from a Galway hearth is beautiful.

And we can't mention *drithle* without giving a shout-out to the Kabin Crew kids from Cork and their song 'The Spark' – 'I searched for my spark and I found it ...' – and it comes from a lovely bit of Baltic ash.

9 MEITHEAMH / 9 JUNE

Boladh bréan
Stench

[bull-a brain]

Tá boladh bréan ag teacht ó leithris na bhfear.
There's an awful smell coming from the men's toilets.

Boladh bréan isn't a phrase for your smelly socks or dog poo on the sole of your shoe. It's not even a smell; it's a stench. The mankiest stink of the highest power.

It reminds me of when my dad brought me to football matches in those old GAA stadiums. There are always steel urinals in the toilets that haven't been cleaned for months and you're gagging trying to go. *Boladh bréan* is the stench of old GAA wee. It's the smell of great men who have relieved themselves there and it's never been flushed.

Some of these stadiums are the pinnacle of GAA greatness. They have the best pitches and goalposts and seated views, but for some reason they've let the toilets go to the dogs. I love the GAA, but they need to do better with their jacks. It doesn't matter if it's a big stadium or your local club with the sound of wee hitting those steel urinals, the smell that builds up over months and years is a right *boladh bréan.*

10 MEITHEAMH / 10 JUNE

Oak
Dair

[dar]

Is crann naofa í an dair sa tír seo.
The oak is a sacred tree of this country.

Oak, the Stabiliser
10 JUNE–7 JULY

If you were born between now and early July, oak is your Celtic tree. Oak trees are the guardians of our island, and people born in the time of this tree are strong and protective. Our tribal ancestors understood trees an awful lot better than we do, which is why there used to be a huge oak forest in Ireland. But we cut them all down for the sake of industry, and now we want them back. If you choose the name Dara for your baby, as thousands of mams and dads do every year, you know where it comes from and that you'll have a strong kid!

11 MEITHEAMH / 11 JUNE

Ciarsúr
Hankie

[keer-suar]

Thairg an fear a chiarsúr don bhean a bhí ag caoineadh ag an tsochraid.
The man offered his hankie to the woman crying at the funeral.

12 MEITHEAMH / 12 JUNE

Bod
Willy

[bud]

Bod ina sheasamh ... Bod ina luí ...
Hard willy ... Soft willy ...

On my first-ever appearance on *The Late Late Show*, back in 2002, I told Pat Kenny all about my *bod*. We had been to Taiwan for the travel show and I'd met a guy in some kung fu master Tai Chi place who could hang 50 kilos off his mickey by using his chi energy. Pat asks, 'Hector, what type of things did you get up to in Asia?' and before I can answer, he says, 'In actual fact, let's have a look.' The tape rolls and there's the big chi energy man hanging a 50-kilo weight off his *bod* and swinging it between his legs, then I hang a 5-kilo weight off my *bod* and swing it between my legs. We were wearing silk skirts, so it was safe for TV.

The clip ends and Pat turns to me: 'Tell us what's going on there exactly, Hector. How is it attached?' Now I'm thinking I'm not going to use the word 'penis' on *The Late Late Show*, so I have to come up with an alternative. You say 'willy' to a child, so what do I use for this situation? The best I could come up with on the spot was *michilín*. The audience understood straight away that I was talking about my mickey and it got a good laugh. Thanks be to God, I thought, because my mother is watching. *Bod* would have been a great alternative if I had thought Pat would understand me, but at least now you know a good word to use if you ever have to say 'penis' on *The Late Late Show*.

13 MEITHEAMH / 13 JUNE

Adharc
Erection

[eye-ark]

Bhí adharc orm ar maidin nuair a dhúisigh mé.
I had an erection this morning when I woke up.

If you have a bod, *you've probably had an* adharc, *so it's good to have both of these in your Irish toolbox.* Adharc *is the Cape of Good Hope – literally, 'the horn'.*

14 MEITHEAMH / 14 JUNE

Míoltóga
Midges

[meel-towg-ah]

Bhí na míoltóga go dona aréir ag an bpáirc peile.
The midges were bad last night at the football pitch.

In my garden in Navan, we had the quintessential row of palm trees that grew to the height of the Empire State Building. And when the football inevitably got lost in them, I'd be the one to have to go in and find it. During the summer, the midges would be out in their billions in the palm trees. It was like the midlands version of a plague of locusts. I'd be eaten alive trying to get the ball back.

There's one particular pitch back West I know from coaching the under-age soccer in Galway, and when you and the lads hear the next match is there, whether it's the under-8s or the under-18s, you think, 'Oh God, no.' Because it's halfway up a hill beside a load of fir trees, and it's on peat bogland, which is just the perfect condition for midges. You're not standing there long before you start scratching your head. No one likes *míoltóga*, but the *míoltóga* seem to like us.

15 MEITHEAMH / 15 JUNE

Preab
Bounce

[prab]

Phreab mé an liathróid.
I bounced the ball.

I learned this verb quickly in the Gaeltacht at the age of eight, because we would play basketball during the cluichí móra (*big games*), *though I would be thinking more about the girls on the team than* ag preabadh na liathróide. Preab *is a vital word for any kids heading to the Gaeltacht this summer.*

16 MEITHEAMH / 16 JUNE

Mótarbhealach
Motorway

[motor-vall-ock]

Chríochnaigh siad an mótarbhealach idir Gaillimh agus Baile Átha Cliath sa bhliain 2009.
They finished the motorway between Galway and Dublin in 2009.

Before we had a *mótarbhealach*, I used to fly from Galway to Dublin three or four times a week. I'd get on an Aer Árann plane at eight o'clock in the morning and by 9.45 a.m. I'd be on Grafton Street.

Back then, if you drove from Galway to Dublin, you would have to go to Oranmore to Craughwell to Athenry, and from there to Ballinasloe and into Athlone. Then it was Kilbeggan to Rochfortbridge and on to Tyrrellspass. When you came to Kinnegad, you wouldn't be far from one of the first plazas in Ireland, before the Age of Applegreens – Mother Hubbards. This was the future of dining while you travel; you would stop there for your sausages and beans and sandwiches and coffee. It was just outside of Enfield, and after your feed it was on to Dublin. The journey took about three-and-a-half hours.

Motorways are brilliant, but it means you don't get to see these towns and villages along the way. There's a bronze statue in the middle of Tyrrellspass that was always a landmark for me, and a whiskey distillery called Locke's in Kilbeggan with its big wooden waterwheel outside. It's a shame people are missing out on seeing these things.

Mótarbhealaí are great for cutting time off your journey, but the badness of them is in the bypass. I take pride in knowing all the nooks and crannies of Ireland because I drove to Dublin before we had the M6.

17 MEITHEAMH / 17 JUNE

Deilf
Dolphin

[delf]

Bhí deilf ag snámh in aice leis an mbád.
There was a dolphin swimming beside the boat.

Back in 2006 I was on the Solimões River in Brazil filming for TG4. We were travelling through South America for three months and we'd just arrived in Brazil from French Guiana. The starting point for our journey was a busy fishing town in the Manaus area. We went to this huge fish market on stilts, where we boarded a traditional longboat with a motor that we would spend the next four days on, heading up the Amazon. As we departed the fish market on the boat, I felt like I was in a scene from *The Mission*.

It was about a three-hour journey to our next stop and we were hammering away up the Amazon, with water coming into the boat and the captain scooping it out again. Rosco, our cameraman, was half asleep and all of a sudden yer man starts pointing to the right. And we see pink dolphins swimming along beside the boat. I've never seen anything like it. They must have followed along with the rhythm of the boat for about 10 minutes. The Amazon is the only place in the world that you can find them, so it was a rare sight for us.

Fungie, our very own Irish *deilf*, was a national treasure until he disappeared. Was he kidnapped? Did he die? There should have been a *Prime Time* special on him. Fungie did wonders for the GDP of Dingle and the government didn't even give him a state funeral.

Min choirce
Ground oats

[minn kwirk-eh]

Is breá linn leite min choirce ar maidin in Éirinn.
We love our porridge in the mornings in Ireland.

19 MEITHEAMH / 19 JUNE

Tuillte
Deserved, earned

[till-cha]

Bhí sé tuillte agat.
You deserved it.

This is a great phrase that can be used in many situations, whether it's in the kitchen, at the gates of the school, at a family reunion, a work do or the dressing room after a match. It's a pat on the back in a word.

20 MEITHEAMH / 20 JUNE

Féileacán
Butterfly

[fail-a-khawn]

Bíonn féileacáin mórthimpeall an ghairdín sa samhradh.
There are butterflies all over the garden in the summer.

I feel like the bees and butterflies of Ireland got an energy boost during Covid, and we were spending more time in our gardens, so we got to see them. It was around this time that my brother Freddie died, and our friend Fiona, who knew Freddie, said, 'You're going to see loads of Freddie around you now, and he's going to come back in the shape of a Red Admiral,' and I said, 'Are you serious? A butterfly?' Fiona is a Celtic-priestessy type of a person and she would be in touch with these things. She told me to particularly keep an eye out in the next few days and weeks.

It's something we do in Ireland when we lose someone – we look for signs of them around us in nature. My mother was always going on about robin redbreasts being a symbol of people who had died. And I'm always watching out for symbols; over the years I've placed them all over my body in the form of tattoos.

I spent a lot of time in my garden after Freddie died, taking comfort in nature, and I swear, there were Red Admirals all over me all summer. One landed on my leg and stayed there for about 10 minutes. It was unbelievable. So then I started talking to the thing, saying, 'I know you're there, Freddie. I know you're around me.' Then I was doing a gig in Kilkenny about two weeks later, and when I arrived in my hotel room, there were two Red Admirals on the window inside the room. I said, 'How are you, Freddie?' and I opened the window for them and they flew out. Looking for these symbols might be something we do in a time of trauma and grief, but it was a chance for me to say hello and smile again, and it made me happy.

21 MEITHEAMH / 21 JUNE
Grianstad an tSamhraidh / Summer Solstice

Breacadh an lae
Daybreak

[brack-a on lay]

Bíonn fear an bhainne amuigh ag breacadh an lae i gcónaí.
The milkman is always out at daybreak.

More and more people go to Newgrange each year for sunrise on the summer solstice. Thousands of people flock there to witness daybreak at the ancient passage tomb; parents bring their kids and hippies bring their drums. It's a beautiful thing.

I celebrated the summer solstice last year with my friends. There were about 40 of us from all over the country – some even came over from Canada and London – and we watched the sun rise on the solstice from our friend's house in the Dublin Mountains. I love that whole 'returning to the land' type of thing and celebrating what Mother Nature has given us. There are little festivals all over the place to mark the solstice, or Bealtaine or something that connects us to ancient Ireland. I think maybe we have become saturated by technology and we're looking for something different.

The people of Slane have always had it cracked; we're just catching up with them. Everyone from Slane is grounded. My friends from Slane all have long hair, smell like patchouli oil and have a great outlook on life. And they love going over the road to Newgrange for *breacadh an lae* on solstice. Our friend Brenda's mother is a Slane hippie and she's been going to India to practise yoga since the 1960s. I can guarantee you that not a single person was doing yoga in Navan in the '60s, but they were doing it in Slane. It's probably because they're so close to Newgrange, Knowth and Dowth – the sacred triangle of ancient Ireland.

22 MEITHEAMH / 22 JUNE

An dól
The dole

[dole]

Nuair a d'fhág mé an scoil, bhí mé ar an dól ar feadh cúpla mí.
When I left school, I was on the dole for a few months.

The dole is an institution of Irish life. It's a rite of passage. I was on it back in the day in Navan, as were many of my mates, and the dole office was run by a lady called Maud. She was a legend in the town – everyone knew her and she knew everyone. The dole office was right beside a real old-style boozer called Fulham's, and on dole day it would be wedged. The pints would be flowing, the coins would be lined up on the pool table and the best pool players in town would be playing.

I remember one Christmas, as an extra boost to the dole, we got butter vouchers. It sounds like real wartime stuff, but it was around 1987 or '88. I gave the vouchers to my mother and she was delighted.

The next time I was *ar an dól* was when I was living on the Aran Islands, and it was dropped off to me every week by Pat John the postman. I was heading to the Féile music festival with my brother Freddie and a few pals that year, and Pat John dropped down the double dole to my door. I hopped on the *Rose of Aran* ferry to the mainland with my double dole in my pocket, and I was so happy, because it meant I would have enough Linden Village cider for the week.

23 MEITHEAMH / 23 JUNE

Péist
Worm

[paysht]

Bhí na páistí ag cuardach péisteanna sa ghairdín.
The children were searching for worms in the garden.

I have an appreciation for worms from living in the countryside, but my favourite type of worm used to be in the bottle of mezcal tequila my brother Freddie would buy us. We were fixated on the idea of finishing the bottle and eating the ceremonial péist *to see if it had a hallucinogenic effect.*

24 MEITHEAMH / 24 JUNE
Lá Fhéile Eoin / Midsummer's Day

Lá Fhéile Eoin
St John's Day

[law ayl-a owen]

Is é Lá Fhéile Eoin croílár an tsamhraidh.
St John's Day is the middle of the summer.

I know when I look out my window on Midsummer's Eve, I'll see smoke from small fires that have been lit all around to symbolise the importance of this night in our calendar. Our ancestors and the ancestors of our European neighbours would have celebrated it every year, and the glow from the fires that I see from my house means that some people have carried on the tradition.

25 MEITHEAMH / 25 JUNE

Colm
Dove

[cull-um]

Bhí díon an tséipéil lán de choilm.
The church roof was full of doves.

Doves are just pigeons with good marketing. They're influencer birds, always making appearances at weddings to get a good photo. But where do they all come from? Where do they live? Does someone own them? Do they have an agent? Because the only time I ever see them is in paintings with Jesus.

I don't know if it has any relation, but I think it's interesting that 'dove' in Irish is *colm*, and we all know someone called Colm – they're our neighbours, our friends, our colleagues. But a flock of *coilm* and a flock of Colms are very different things. You'd never release a flock of Colms at your wedding – they're only ever to be seen in a pub on a Saturday night drinking pints of Heineken.

26 MEITHEAMH / 26 JUNE

Meacan bán
Parsnip

[mea-khan bawn]

Ní féidir dinnéar an Domhnaigh a ithe gan chairéid agus meacain bhána.
You can't have a Sunday dinner without carrots and parsnips.

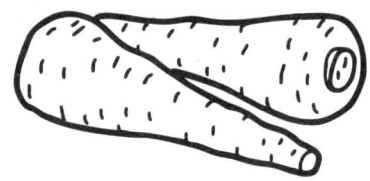

27 MEITHEAMH / 27 JUNE

Humas
Hummus

[hum-ass]

Ní thuigim humas.
I don't get hummus.

Who brought hummus to Ireland? They've a lot to answer for. Someone is making a lot of money out of pots of hummus and I don't think we really need it to survive. The Birkenstocks-and-mullet brigade are gathering momentum all over the world, and they're bringing humas *with them. They have to be stopped.*

28 MEITHEAMH / 28 JUNE

An mhéar láir
The middle finger

[on vayr lawr]

Ag na soilse tráchta, fuair mé an mhéar láir ó tiománaí.
I got the middle finger off a driver at the traffic lights.

It used to be the two fingers, and there was no real meanness or danger in it, but then the 'shove it up your hole' one-fingered salute arrived on the scene. An mhéar láir is the secret weapon of the angry driver, and they always have to do a face with it.

29 MEITHEAMH / 29 JUNE

Coincleach/Caonach liath
Mould

[cwin-clach]

Bhí coincleach ar an mballa sa seomra folctha.
There was mould on the wall in the bathroom.

We've all seen it. We've all rented an apartment with it. Some of us have grown up with it. When I think of this word, I can practically hear the sound of the extractor fan in the windowless bathroom. The air might be fine for a while, but soon enough you see the coincleach *on the ceiling.*

30 MEITHEAMH / 30 JUNE

Staonaire
Teetotaller

[stain-er-a]

Níor ól sé deoch ariamh; is staonaire ceart é m'uncail.
He never drank a drop; my uncle is a real teetotaller.

Before the designated driver, there was the teetotaller. I have complete respect for the people who choose to not touch a drop of alcohol. My uncle Micheál was one – he was a teetotaller who loved a cup of tea.

The closest I came to being a teetotaller was getting my Pioneer pin at my Confirmation. I took what was called 'the pledge'. But I blew the pledge out of the water when I was 16 in the Russell Arms Hotel in Navan.

There was a good load of lads from school there and we were all sitting down the back, as far away from the bar as possible. We ordered Harp, because it was a man's drink. And the keg probably didn't have to travel far to Navan, because it was brewed 40-odd miles away in Dundalk. I vividly remember the six golden towers of bubbly alcohol sitting on the table in front of us. And I didn't rush it; the pledge slipped away with every nice slow sip of Harp.

Then when I moved from Navan to Dublin, I graduated from Harp to a more sophisticated beverage: Furstenberg. Since then I've broken my pledge a fair few times, so I'm no *staonaire*.

1 IÚIL / 1 JULY

Uachtar gréine
Suncream

[ookh-ter gray-nya]

Rinne mé dearmad ar uachtar gréine inné; tá mé dóite.
I forgot the suncream yesterday; I'm burned.

The only time you put on suncream in Navan in the 1970s was when you went to Bettystown, the Riviera of Meath. We'd pile into the car and Dad would always stop at Kentstown, where there was a statue of a lion's head spouting water from its mouth. He'd say, 'Right, get out of the car. We're going to drink from the lion's head.' I thought the water was magic.

We'd get to the beach and my mother would get us dressed in our togs. She'd pull on my tight stripey purple Speedos, even though I was about eight. Then she'd slather on the *uachtar gréine*. It would be so thick it would look like whey protein. Me and my brothers Freddie and Mark would sit on a big tartan rug – not even a blanket – on the sand dunes. The sea would be so far out that we'd have to walk about a mile and a half to get to it, and then the sun would go behind a cloud and you'd be freezing. We'd all go to the Neptune Hotel for lunch, which to me was like going to a five-star casino in Monaco. We'd have a sandwich and a bowl of soup, even though it was a hot day.

Then we'd stop on the way back from the beach in Duleek in the Greyhound Bar for a red lemonade and a packet of crisps, all smiling and tired and smelling of *uachtar gréine*. To me, the smell of suncream will always be the smell of the seaside, even when I'm rubbing the Factor 50 onto my translucent Irish skin in the back of a HiAce in Alice Springs in Australia or Addis Ababa in Ethiopia.

2 IÚIL / 2 JULY

Gliomach
Lobster

[glyum-okh]

Tharraing an t-iascaire an pota gliomach isteach sa churrach.
The fisherman pulled the lobster pot into the currach.

3 IÚIL / 3 JULY

Faoileán
Seagull

[fway-lawn]

Tá na faoileáin in Éirinn ar na faoileáin is raimhre ar domhan.
The seagulls in Ireland are amongst the fattest seagulls in the world.

Seagulls are in abundance in places like Bundoran and Castletownbere and Salthill. They're huge Atlantic gulls fattened from the abundance of waste and overflowing dustbins on our cities' streets. Between 3 a.m. and 6 a.m., dinner is served: half-eaten pizzas, leftover cod and chips, snack boxes. They feast on these culinary delights and use car parks as their Airbnbs, sheltered from the wind and the rain. And then they're back at lunchtime to rob a bag of chips right out of your hands. A tourist eating an ice cream is just a target to a seagull.

People who travel to Thailand or Indonesia are fascinated when a local monkey trots over and steals their lunch, but monkeys are just the seagulls of South East Asia. We should turn the tables and start posting videos of seagulls robbing sandwiches and tell Americans that it's good luck. They have the famous Monkey Temple in Ubud in Bali, so we should have the *Faoileán* Temple in the Claddagh.

4 IÚIL / 4 JULY

Poncán
Yank

[punk-awn]

Tá aithne againn ar fad ar an bponcán sa scannán The Field *le Richard Harris.*
We all know the Yank in the film *The Field* with Richard Harris.

Are we the only people in the world who call Americans 'Yanks'? The word conjures up an image of the lad coming over from Boston to trace his roots or John Wayne boxing those men over a bridge in Connemara in The Quiet Man.

5 IÚIL / 5 JULY

Lag
Weak

[log]

Bhí mé tinn inné, mhothaigh mé lag.
I was sick yesterday, I felt weak.

Lag can be used for the physical feeling of weakness or for a weak performance in sport. And now that it's July, you might even be feeling weak with the heat.

6 IÚIL / 6 JULY

Port techno
Techno tune

[purt tek-no]

Is breá liom cúpla poirt techno maith agus mé ag tiomáint sa charr.
I love a few good techno tunes when I'm driving in the car.

I used to run an underground techno club back in the day called Bubble. They were one-off nights in the Eglinton Hotel in Galway from 1994 to 1997-ish. My friends doing Art in Galway College would make these psychedelic backdrops for the stage and I'd bring down all the cool DJs from Dublin to play techno tunes. Once I brought an ice cream van in the door at around two in the morning and gave out ice pops. It was pretty cool.

My real love of techno and hard house started at a nightclub called The Sex Kitchen in The Castle – it was Galway's version of The Haçienda in Manchester, Sir Henry's in Cork and The Ormond in Dublin. They had the likes of Tall Paul, Carl Cox, Sasha, John Digweed and Darren Emerson. It was phenomenal.

I met loads of my best mates dancing to techno at these nights, and they were all from Ballinrobe. We're all older now, but we'll still get together the odd time to let the hair down, and every time The Prodigy comes on, I start singing 'Mayo People, Voodoo People' to them, because Mayo people love a banging *port techno*.

7 IÚIL / 7 JULY

Draíocht
Magic

[dree-okht]

Bhí draíocht álainn faoin tuath.
There was a beautiful magic in the countryside.

I was filming a show about the occult in England, and we were going for a bit of a magical, mystical vibe – druids, fortune tellers and the like. We arranged to meet a load of white witches who were heading deep into the woods for a ceremony. In my mind, there would be offerings to the gods, initiation rituals, chanting around a big fire, blood offerings and even the possibility of a vestal virgin, which came straight from my love of *Robin Hood*, *Herne the Hunter*, *Vikings* and all of that.

Well, about six people turned up, the wood was a half a mile off the M3, the fire was shite and the chanting was boring – there wasn't a hint of an ancient language. I was disappointed, to say the least.

After 10 minutes of this, I knew if we weren't getting any *Wicker Man* vibes, we'd have to make them ourselves, so I proposed a dream-like sequence to the crew; something you'd see in a horror movie. The idea was to take my kit off and dart through the forest like a frightened deer, while they filmed my naked body on a long lens. We all thought this would be a good shout, so I undressed behind a large tree away from everyone, and … 'Action!' My naked body swept through the vegetation, stalked and hunted.

When the show went out, my mother called me: 'Why in the name of God did you have to take your clothes off and run through the forest? Jesus Christ almighty!' Turns out there's nothing magical about my bare arse on national television.

8 IÚIL / 8 JULY

Crann cuilinn
Holly

[krown kwill-in]

Tá an pháirc in aice liom lán de chrainn chuilinn.
The park beside me is full of holly trees.

Holly, the Ruler
8 JULY–4 AUGUST

If you were born between now and early August, your Celtic tree is the holly. It seems like an odd one for the middle of summer, with most of us thinking about holly around Christmas, but they're evergreens, so you'll see it in parks and hedges most of the year. It's a strong tree, and the people born in the time of the holly are ambitious and good leaders. *Cuilinn* appears in some Irish place names as well. In English, 'Moycullen' is meaningless, but *Maigh Cuilinn* means 'The Plain of Holly' – beautiful!

9 IÚIL / 9 JULY

Miotasach
Mythical

[myut-aws-okh]

Tá scéalta miotasacha ar fud na háite i stair na hÉireann.
There are mythical stories all over the place in Irish history.

When you're born in Navan, you're born only about 10 miles from the Hill of Tara, but I never really knew what a powerful place it was until I was older. It was only through my travels to the other side of the world that I realised the significance of Tara and the richness we have in Irish legends.

I was in the back of our van in Bangladesh when a song came on and I kept hearing the word 'Tara' over and over again. I asked the driver if I was right and, he said yes, that it's an important word in Hindu culture. It means 'star'. There is also a goddess Tara in Hindu and, it turns out, in Buddhism as well. Then when I spent time with the Māori in New Zealand, I came across the phrase 'Te Ara', pronounced 'tara', which means 'the pathway'. How in the name of God does 'Tara' mean so many spiritual things all over the world, and it was right on my doorstep in Navan?

When I was with the Aboriginal peoples in Australia, I learned that so much of their culture is about ancient stories and mythologies – it's in the landscape, their songs, their language. It is threaded through their way of life, and with it comes great respect for their elders, who pass these stories down to the next generation. Why isn't it like that here? Every county in Ireland has a rich vault of mythology that should be unearthed and taught at national school. Parents should be telling their children the story of the goddess Boann when they're crossing the Boyne and the story of the Cailleach when they're on their holidays in Dingle. It should go beyond Cú Chulainn – there's so much in these *miotasach* stories that connect us to our past.

10 IÚIL / 10 JULY

Cráin dhubh
Orca (Killer whale)

[krawn ghuv]

Chonaic mé scannán faisnéise faoin gcráin dhubh ar Discovery an lá cheana.
I saw a documentary on orcas on Discovery the other day.

11 IÚIL / 11 JULY

Leisciúil
Lazy

[lesh-kyool]

Bhí lá leisciúil agam inné, mar ní raibh mé ag obair.
I had a lazy day yesterday, as I wasn't at work.

'Lazy' is a teacher's favourite word for the school report. The education system associates it with being 'bad', but is being lazy not a talent? Just because a child has their chin in their hands doesn't mean they're disinterested; their body is just telling them, 'This is the way I feel at the moment.' Look at lions – they lie around all day, but what else are you going to do in the midday sun in the Serengeti? They're being efficient with their energy.

There are some people who are incapable of being lazy – they're 'go-go-go!' all the time, but it's a skill to be able to switch off. It's a lovely feeling to just say, 'Well, feck you all anyway', knock off the alarm and turn over in the bed. Isn't it lovely when we see our children having a little snooze? So let's not be slaves to the system. We can be *leisciúil* for one part of the day and get the work done after.

12 IÚIL / 12 JULY

Maitrís
Matrix

[mah-treesh]

Thaitin an scannán An Mhaitrís *go mór liom.*
I loved *The Matrix* film.

Here's a quirky one for you. You might think you don't need to know the word for 'matrix' in Irish, but if Laurence Fishburne walks into a pub in Connemara and asks you and the aul lads at the bar, '*Ar chuala sibh faoin maitrís?*' (Have you heard about the matrix?), you'll know to ignore him and turn back to your pints of Guinness. I'd say there's many a person in Connemara who drank poitín and saw the matrix. Poitín can turn a man inside out and back in again. Maybe that's what the film was *really* about.

When the film came out, Irish speakers probably just put a 'h' after the 'm' in 'Matrix' and pronounced it 'Waytrix': '*An bhfaca tú An Mhatrix?*' (Did you see *The Matrix*?). The word *maitrís* is a relatively new one for the Irish language, but poitín has been around for hundreds of years, so there were probably monks on Skellig Michael who saw the *maitrís* but didn't know what to call it.

13 IÚIL / 13 JULY

Gráinnín gainimh
Grain of sand

[graw-neen gon-yuv]

Bíonn gráinnín gainimh i ngach áit théis na trá.
There are grains of sand everywhere after the beach.

Gráinnín gainimh is such a lovely phrase to say. It almost sings off the page: 'graaaw-neen gon-yuv'. It's the tiny little grain of sand you find on your favourite local beach, millions of them sliding through your fingers when you pick up a handful.

I was in Broom in the north of Australia, and it was the centre of mother-of-pearl production in the world for a hundred years. Aboriginal people used to dive for the huge oysters that were in abundance in the coral reefs. I got to spend time with some of the Aboriginals on their coastal lands, and I found an oyster. When we opened up its massive shell, there was a little crab running around inside. Apparently, all oysters have a little crab who lives in the shell and acts as a landlord, keeping the place tidy. I could see the full biology of the oyster inside. There's the oyster meat, and in the middle of the organs is the gonad. The Aboriginal guy told me to rub my finger on it, and I could feel something inside. So he gives me a tiny little knife and when I cut it open, out pops a perfect white pearl. And he told me how they're made.

If a little grain of sand gets inside the shell and the oyster can't get it out, it starts to coat the grain in fluid. Layer after layer of fluid is wrapped around this sand and it eventually hardens and forms a beautiful pearl.

Pearls always remind me of my mother, and all mammies in Ireland who would keep their pearl necklaces in their jewellery boxes and only wear them to mass on Sunday or for a special occasion. It was amazing to know that each of the pearls on my mother's necklace was formed from a single *gráinnín gainimh*.

14 IÚIL / 14 JULY

Ollmhór
Gigantic

[ull-wore]

Is stát ollmhór é Western Australia.
Western Australia is a gigantic state.

There's only one way to describe Australia, and it's 'fucking gigantic'. When I was there in 2006, I didn't really appreciate how big it was, but when I went back for the travel show in 2025, I realised it's humongous. It's about 36 times the size of Ireland. Perth is the capital of Western Australia and it is the most remote major city in the world. You would have to travel over 2,000 kilometres to reach the next major city, so you don't really go to Western Australia to visit; you go there to live. It has to be seen to be believed. It was like the final frontier.

I was about three hours south of Perth in a middle-of-nowhere Mary Hick town called Williams. It had a petrol station, a shop and a saloon-type hotel called The Williams Hotel. We stopped there at about ten o'clock on a Saturday night to get a bit of rest, and when we walked into the only pub in town, the barman greeted me in Irish. He was from Claregalway, my village. Then six or seven people turned around and said in Irish accents, 'Hector, what are you doing here?' I said, 'What the fuck are *you* doing here?' They were all young people out in Australia working on farms, driving big machinery. Even in the middle of nowhere in a state as *ollmhór* as Western Australia, I managed to find Irish people.

15 IÚIL / 15 JULY

Ag pléascadh
Bursting

[egg play-ska]

Bhí mé ag pléascadh le dul chuig an leithreas ar maidin ag an gcruinniú.
I was bursting for the toilet this morning at the meeting.

Everyone knows this feeling. You're in a meeting and you're dying for a wee so much that it's almost leaving your body. If you're about to erupt in your jocks, you're *ag pléascadh*.

I've been *ag pléascadh* many times, but none more so than when me and my brother Freddie were hitching back to Dublin from Navan one Sunday evening. I knew I was sort of half-bursting to go to the toilet, but when you have your thumb out hitching and there's not a single tree or lamp-post to wee behind, you just have to hold it. There was no way I was weeing in the sacred River Boyne.

A driver picked us up and by the time we got to Dunboyne, I was bursting. I couldn't really ask this lad to stop the car after picking us up, so I just sucked it back into my willy as best I could. We hit traffic all the way in by the Phoenix Park, past the Ashtown Tin Box, and on to the Navan Road, which goes on for about 27 miles. I was looking at all the landmarks going, 'How long? How much longer?' I could see the big church near our road in the distance and I knew we were nearly there ...

I managed to get out of the car, walk down the alleyway to our bedsit, turn the key in the door ... but as soon as my feet hit the stairs, my bladder surrendered. I had been bursting for the last 56 minutes and I just stood there and weed in my tight, whitewashed Levis. By the time I got to the toilet on the second floor, there was nothing left. Now that's the definition of *ag pléascadh*.

16 IÚIL / 16 JULY

Díon gréine
Sunroof

[dee-an gray-nya]

Bhí díon gréine ar charr mo dhaidí fadó.
My dad's car years ago had a sunroof.

A sunroof in a car in the 1970s and '80s was the be-all and end-all. When your father put the hand up and pulled the sunroof back, it was bliss. Who decided to cut a hole in the roof of a car and make it luxury? The díon gréine *was a great invention.*

17 IÚIL / 17 JULY

Galar
Disease

[gaw-lar]

Bhí go leor galar thart ag tús an naoú haois déag.
There was lots of disease around at the beginning of the nineteenth century.

Irish people have come through many galair, *from the bubonic plague to tuberculosis. It's not exactly a nice word, but you can flip it as well*: i ngalar an ghrá *means 'infected with love' or 'love-smitten'.*

18 IÚIL / 18 JULY

Tairne
Nail

[tarn-ya]

Bhí an tairne san adhmad lán de mheirg.
The nail in the wood was full of rust.

19 IÚIL / 19 JULY

Tatú
Tattoo

[tattoo]

Fuair mé mo chéad tatú sa Mint i leataobh ó Shráid Uí Mhórdha i mBaile Átha Cliath fadó.
I got my first tattoo in The Mint off Moore St in Dublin years ago.

When I was in New Zealand for the travel show, I was invited to witness a Māori tattoo ceremony. Tattoos are really important in Māori culture, and facial tattoos are probably the most symbolic of them. They get different types of tattoos when they reach different milestones in their lives.

I got to see a *moko kauae* ceremony, where a woman journeying into her late twenties got a chin tattoo. I never realised that the type of tattoo you get in Māori culture usually says something about what type of person you are – so, if you are a good speaker, you might have a bird near your mouth. Your tattoo says something about how your family sees you. This particular woman was being tattooed by her mother, and she got a series of lines on her chin while she held a sacred green stone called the *pounamu*.

These *moko* are so important in Māori culture that there can be no discrimination against them any more in New Zealand – you see accountants, doctors, teachers, people from all walks of life with *tatúnna* on their faces.

20 IÚIL / 20 JULY

Slog siar é
Knock it back

[slug sheer ay]

Bhí round de Baby Guinnesses os comhair na leaids: 'Slog siar é!'
There was a round of baby Guinnesses in front of the lads: 'Knock it back!'

Who came up with the idea of a Baby Guinness? There's not been a hen party in history in Carrick-on-Shannon that hasn't come back from the bar with a big tray of them. And if you do buy a round, you better have a few quid in your pocket, because they're not cheap, and then they're down the hatch in three seconds. They're a publican's dream, and they don't even have Guinness in them.

My mother, Trina, had her first Baby Guinness at Christmas 2016 at the age of 73, and she thought it was the best thing ever invented. She didn't even want to drink it, she just wanted to have her picture taken with it. She sat there sipping it for about an hour. I doubt Trina ever knocked anything back, but then she was never in The Royal Meath pub at 11:30 at night with a full pint in front of her when the minibus to the Ardboyne Hotel was about to leave. The only way to make sure you make it to Diamonds nightclub in that situation is to *slog siar é*.

21 IÚIL / 21 JULY

Cúlchaint
Gossip

[kool-kynt]

Bhí go leor cúlchaint ar siúl sa pharóiste faoin scéal sin.
There was a lot of gossip going on in the parish about that story.

Cúlchaint *translates directly to 'behind-talk' in English. We love a bit of gossip in Ireland – we were reared on it – but the Irish phrase reminds us that it's really just talking behind someone's back, so we should stay away from it.*

22 IÚIL / 22 JULY

Púic tae
Tea cosy

[pu-ik tay]

Bhí púic tae ag Mrs Doyle sa sraith teilifíse Father Ted.
Mrs Doyle had a tea cosy on the TV series *Father Ted*.

Back in 2005, I travelled to New Zealand to shoot a documentary about the Lions Rugby Tour. Pauline McLynn happened to be on our flight home. I knew Pauline through work, so we had a few drinks at the airport before our night flight out of Auckland to Los Angeles, and that continued on the plane, as you do. Halfway through the flight, the purser, a gregarious Kiwi, recognised Pauline. He was a massive *Father Ted* fan and so photos were taken and champagne was produced from first class. By this stage, most of the cabin crew had met Mrs Doyle, and as the lights were dimmed for night-time, the purser asked a favour of Pauline for the next day ...

Morning came around and Pauline made good on her promise. She got on the intercom as breakfast was being served – in full Mrs Doyle mode. Now think about it: you have been asleep through the night, you're feeling a bit groggy, the intercom goes 'DING DONG!' and you hear Mrs Doyle from *Father Ted* telling everyone what's on the menu and that tea and coffee and more tea will be served: 'Ahhhh go on, go on, go on, ye will all have a cup of tea!' Frowns of disbelief all around me, eyes squinting in confusion, 'What the fuck? Is that Mrs Doyle?'

'Mrs Doyle' then proceeded to walk down the aisle and serve a few teas and coffees. It was a surreal moment, 39,000 feet above the Pacific Ocean. Even the captain came on the intercom to thank Mrs Doyle for serving tea on the flight that morning. The plane erupted in applause. All she was missing was the *púic tae*.

23 IÚIL / 23 JULY

Ag téacsáil
Texting

[egg tex-awl]

Ná bí ag téacsáil is tú ag tiomáint.
Don't text and drive at the same time.

WhatsApp has revolutionised texting for men in their 40s and 50s. They have no interest in being in the local youth club WhatsApp groups getting notifications about their kids, but it has opened up a community for groups of pals, who can send off a quick message every day, even if they rarely see each other in real life. Because we don't pick up the phone to say, 'Hello, Phil. Long time, no see. How's things in Cardiff?', WhatsApp groups for men are the digital version of a pint in the pub.

There are about 20 of us in my man-friend WhatsApp group. We're all best pals (even though I haven't seen some of them in ages because they live in Glasgow or Newfoundland) and when we get into a rhythm of texting and there are 40 messages flying in and out from all over the world, I get a great kick out of it.

I've honed my skills *téacsála* in these middle-aged men's WhatsApp groups. I think I'm fairly nifty at this stage. I'm not as quick as a 16-year-old, but for my age group I'm pretty good. If there was an over-50s texting championship, I'd be right up there. I can imagine it being held in the Longford Arms Hotel, like something from *Killinaskully*. 'Aaaaand representing Galway for the over-50s, we have Hector Ó hEochagáin!

24 IÚIL / 24 JULY

Gairleog
Garlic

[garl-yowg]

Tá cumhacht faoi leith ag an ngairleog.
Garlic has powerful strength.

I don't remember having garlic in the house when we were growing up. I'd say Navan was the last town to get it when Irish households discovered it. Someone in the fruit and veg market in Smithfield in Dublin must have had a notion in 1983 to import garlic from Greece or somewhere. Then it appeared on the shelves in Quinnsworth and became an instrumental flavour in our dinners. There are even different strains of garlic in supermarkets – white and pink and purple bulbs (that all taste the same).

I think we all have a special little place in our kitchens where we keep our garlic. In ours, it's a little wicker basket that I got when I was in Ho Chi Minh City that we store our garlic and ginger in. The trick is to use it all before it starts sprouting shoots and turns into something from the *Little Shop of Horrors*. But we all have our garlic presses and know how to cook with it. It's a staple ingredient and we wouldn't be without it. We are spud people in Ireland, but we are *gairleog* people now too.

25 IÚIL / 25 JULY

Friochtán
Frying pan

[frukh-tawn]

Déan dearmad ar d'aerfhriochtóir; ní féidir gan friochtán a bheith agat sa bhaile.
Forget your air fryer; no home can do without a frying pan.

26 IÚIL / 26 JULY

Íseal

Low

[ee-shall]

Fuair sé an liathróid agus sháigh sé go híseal isteach i gcúinne na heangaí í.
He got the ball and stuck it low into the corner of the net.

You will find íseal *in the phrase in* ísle brí (*meaning 'at a low ebb'*) *from my first book,* The Irish Words You Should Know. Íseal *means low in any way, whether emotional or physical. Every time the great Gaelic footballer David Clifford scores, it's low into the corner of the net.* Íseal *is his style.*

27 IÚIL / 27 JULY

Teach soghluaiste
Mobile home

[tyokh so-gloosh-ta]

Is breá leis na hÉireannaigh teach soghluaiste ag an gcósta.
Irish people love a mobile home on the coast.

We have been going to a mobile home in Lahinch for decades. Lahinch is *Leacht Uí Chonchubhair* in Irish – the Cairn of O'Connor – so the English version is meaningless. My mother-in-law has had a mobile home there for 40 years, and then all the siblings chipped in to get a new one. Our kids were reared there over the summers on cold-meat salads and Miwadi. But we've upgraded in recent years: we got a patio out the front during the decking boom of the Celtic Tiger and now it even has an en suite.

There's something satisfying about watching an All-Ireland Final on your phone from the mobile home because there's no satellite, then going outside in the 16-degree heat to look at the grey skies and having a glass of white wine. I think there's nothing nicer than being in a *teach soghluaiste* near the beach in the middle of winter in Ireland. You can look out at the crashing sea and the long beach, and it's just majestic.

28 IÚIL / 28 JULY

Coill
Wood

[kwill]

Tá coill álainn taobh thiar den teach inar rugadh mé.
There's a lovely wood behind the house where I was born.

Coill is the word for that small wood we all know, the one not far from your house, or near a cousin's house that you went to all the time. It's the lovely little place you could go to get lost as a child and return to years later with your own children and still feel at home there.

29 IÚIL / 29 JULY

Fánaí
Rambler

[faw-nee]

Chuaigh grúpa fánaithe suas an sliabh inné.
A group of ramblers went up the mountain yesterday.

I have respect for ramblers, the ones who can walk the Wicklow Way no bother, but I don't know what to make of the ones with the brand-new boots and thick socks and their water flask yokes. You can use this word for someone who rambles on when they're talking too: 'He was a real *fánaí*.'

30 IÚIL / 30 JULY

Bruitíneach
Measles

[britch-eeh-nokh]

Bhíodh an bhruitíneach na blianta ó shin.
Measles was very common years ago.

This reminds me of the famous MMR vaccination. We all had to pull up our sleeves in national school and get the whack in the arm. I know in some schools back in the day, you were even rewarded with a sugar lump to ease the pain. Thanks to that, it was bye-bye bruitíneach.

31 IÚIL / 31 JULY

Ag tafann
Barking

[egg toff-in]

Bhí an madra ag tafann ar feadh na hoíche.
The dog was barking all night.

Our Jack Russell's bark isn't deep, but it's still loud. When he sees or hears something, he's on it, ag tafann, *even if it's four in the morning. It's enough to make me get out of bed in the nip to let him out.*

1 LÚNASA / 1 AUGUST

Ceiliúradh
Celebration

[kell-oor-ah]

Bhí ceiliúradh mór ag an gclann.
The family had a big celebration.

A community get-together, a tribal get-together or a family get-together – a *ceiliúradh* is something you don't want to miss. It's a celebration that excites you, that you mark down in the calendar in anticipation. It's not the invitation you get to a wedding and think, 'Ah God, we'll have to go to that wedding. It's not the same Saturday as the match, is it?' You don't *have* to be at a *ceiliúradh*, you *want* to be at a *ceiliúradh*. You know it will have the right people and the right atmosphere, so you'll have an unbelievable time.

The entire month of August is an ancient Irish *ceiliúradh*. Lughnasa is the start of the harvest, the celebration of a time of bounty, merriment and rituals. It's one of the four powerful Celtic yearly festivals and its name comes from the legendary god Lugh, a fierce womaniser and warrior who loved life and loved a party. He wanted the tribes and his people to let their hair down and celebrate this time of year. If Lugh arrived at Electric Picnic, he would head straight for the Body & Soul area. He was a *ceiliúradh* master.

2 LÚNASA / 2 AUGUST

Fionnuar
Cool/trendy

[fyun-oo-ar]

Beidh Paul Weller fionnuar i gcónaí.
Paul Weller will always be cool.

Fionnuar wasn't on my radar until a few years ago. It has to have been created by the new wave of Irish speakers. You just wouldn't get a 60- or 70-year-old man walking into a pub in Connemara and saying, '*Sláinte*! This place is very cool, isn't it?' I don't know what they would have said, but that's the beauty of language. There are new words added to the dictionary every year to reflect the world, and now in Irish you can talk about how you thought a film on Netflix was *fionnuar*.

It makes me think of Paul Weller. I've always loved him, from the earliest days of The Jam through to The Style Council and then into his own solo world of Weller. He always stood out with the sharp lines of his clothes. It was the mod look with the Harrington jackets, the parkas, the locks in the hair, the tonic suits, the Lambretta scooters. A few years back I met the lads from The Small Faces, who along with The Who were the bands at the epicentre of the UK mod scene at the tail end of the 1960s. We were in Soho and 20 or 30 mods turned up in full gear on the coolest, most pimped-out Lambrettas you've ever seen. It was like the movie *Quadrophenia* all over again. London has always been a mod town and always will be. Mods will never die, because modern culture is never not in fashion and it's always *fionnuar*.

3 LÚNASA / 3 AUGUST

Mún; Múnlann
Urine; Urinal

[moo-in; moo-in-lawn]

Bhí mé ag pléascadh. Mar sin rinne mé mún taobh thiar de chrann.
I was bursting. So I did a wee-wee behind a tree.

Me and the missus travelled for many years to Roskilde, the Danish version of Glastonbury. It's three days of an eclectic mix of bands, proper local Carlsberg beer and over 100,000 Scandinavians. I love my metal music, and when I was there around 1999 the opening day was a real treat: we saw Ministry, Monster Magnet and Metallica. The vibe and layout of the festival blew our minds. No beer queues at the bar, just crates of cold bottled beer everywhere, and if you brought the crate of empties back, you got a discount on the next crate. There were hot showers in the campsite, superb food stalls, and the best thing of all was the abundance of toilets. Even three days into the festival, the toilets were reasonably clean, unlike every Irish festival where the Portaloos turn into a horror show of puke, shit and wee. Throw in the rain and muck, and the journey at 5 a.m. from your tent to the toilet for a number two is an experience, to say the least.

The Danes have been leading the way in many areas for years – clothes, furniture, lighting and, of course, Lego – but for the first time, I was really taken aback by the smart thinking at Roskilde. Turns out they could keep the jacks so clean and avoid queues because they attached a rubber urinal type thing to the base of the big trees that were all over the campsite and stage areas. They protected the trees as well as preventing the areas of greenery from becoming piss swamps. Because, as we all know, when one lad sees another lad go against a tree, all of a sudden 25 lads are over doing a *mún*.

4 LÚNASA / 4 AUGUST

Neadar
Not sure/Who knows?

[nya-dar]

– *An bhfuil tú ag dul go dtí an ócáid oibre?*
– *Neadar.*
– Are you going to go to that work do?
– Not sure.

When you don't know whether to say yes or no, when you're not really pushed, it's neadar. *It's a get-out-of-jail-free card when you really want to say no. It's indecision in a nutshell.*

5 LÚNASA / 5 AUGUST

Crann coill
Hazel tree

[krawn kwill]

Is é an crann coill an crann Ceilteach duitse.
Your Celtic tree is the hazel tree.

Hazel, the Knower
5 AUGUST–1 SEPTEMBER

The hazel is my Celtic horoscope tree. It's a tree that I've always had around me, but I never knew its significance. Those of us born under the hazel are said to have great memories. I'm not great with remembering people's names, but I think I have a good memory of landmarks and places I've been. It's an attribute I'm proud to have.

Years ago, when we moved into our house, we had to do something about the three orange Wavin pipes that were jutting out of the ground where you have your sewage tank. Anyone who has bought a house in the countryside knows all about this. You walk into your lovely house for the first time, delighted that you're finally in, then you look out the back garden and it's just a load of flattened soil with three massive pipes sticking up. It still looks like a building site. So I put a load of soil around the Wavin pipes and made a whole new flower bed, and I planted bamboo to sort of disguise the pipes. And then this other tree started growing out of one of the bamboo pots ...

Brenda, our hedge witch friend who knows all about Celtic horoscopes, came around and said, 'That's a hazel tree. Did you plant that?' 'No,' I said, and she goes, 'Well that's your Celtic tree.' The hazel had pushed itself up around the bamboo and the Wavin pipes. I didn't know anything about the Celtic tree horoscope before that, but since then I've always had a hazel in the garden.

6 LÚNASA / 6 AUGUST

Gráinneog
Hedgehog

[graw-nyowg]

Ní fheiceann tú gráinneoga mórán, ach tá siad ann.
You don't see too many hedgehogs, but they are out there.

7 LÚNASA / 7 AUGUST

Préachán
Crow

[pray-a-khawn]

Tagann na préacháin le chéile i gcónaí roimh an gcith báistí.
Crows always come together before the shower of rain.

Crows, magpies and seagulls are the mafia of Ireland's birds. If there was a préachán *cartel, it would probably be the most powerful mob in Ireland. It's not called a murder of crows for nothing.*

8 LÚNASA / 8 AUGUST

Fobhríste
Underpants

[fo-bhree-shteh]

Fadó fadó, cheannaíodh mo mháthair fobhrístí dom in Penneys san Uaimh.
Years ago, my mother used to buy my underpants in Penneys in Navan.

What I didn't envision happening as a dad of two young men was that my jocks would become their jocks. They wouldn't dream of wearing Penneys jocks – it's all about the name, so there's a plethora of Hugo Boss and Calvin Kleins around the house. I would never have dared wear my father's jocks or even let them near my nether regions. He wore the old-style Y-fronts, real men's jocks that were worn for days.

So when Tommy Tiernan and I had to do a photo shoot back in 2009 to promote our new show on iRadio, I wanted to pay homage to the greatness of the *fobhrístí* of my father's generation. The show was a bit mad and we wanted to do something different for the publicity campaign, so for the photo, me and Tommy decided to lie on a luxurious leather couch together in nothing but our jocks. We must have tried on six different kinds of underpants, but in the end, a pair of tight, white Y-fronts did the job. The photo was taken and it went up on billboards all around the country. I was so excited that someone I knew would be driving along the motorway or a main road in town and see me in my bright white *fobhríste*. As far as I was concerned, if you get on a billboard in Ireland, you've made it.

9 LÚNASA / 9 AUGUST

Uaireadóir
Watch

[oor-a-dor]

Fuair mé mo chéad uaireadóir digiteach do mo Chóineartú.
I got my first digital watch for my Confirmation.

I was 12 years old when I got my first watch. Having a digital watch was all the rage at the time. The idea that you pushed a button and you could see the date, and if you pushed another one, the watch would light up! I had my eye on this black-and-gold one in a jewellery shop called Town Jewellers on the main street. At that age, when you saw something that you wanted in the window of a shop, you'd stare at it and hope someone else wouldn't buy it.

My dad knew the people in there. We had our drapery shop a few doors down from the jewellers, right across from St Mary's Church at the heart of Trimgate Street. Everyone knew everyone back then in Navan, and Trimgate Street was the shopping epicentre of the town – you could get anything you needed. There was China Garden; Paddy Fitzsimon's bar; Geoghegan's across the road, which was like a rural Arnotts; Dunnes Stores; Fitzpatrick's newsagents; Hyland's garage; Steen O'Reilly solicitors; then the greatest sports and shoe shop of all time, Jacksie Kiernan's, where Jacksie himself sold Meath jerseys and all the training gear. Beside Jacksie's was Gallagher's sweet shop, then it was the post office, and we're right back to the Town Jewellers, where I stood outside staring at the sleek black-and-gold digital watch of my dreams ... and my dad bought it for me for my Confirmation.

I loved that watch. It was vintage, as we say in Navan. I played with the torch every night under my blanket, checking the time and date. And when I wore my Confirmation suit, if I extended my arm just right, the sleeve would pull up and there it was in all its glory: my digital *uaireadóir*.

10 LÚNASA / 10 AUGUST

An Mhór-Roinn
The Continent

[on voor-ryn]

Chuaigh mé ar saoire an mhála droma ar an Mór-Roinn ar feadh bliana sna nóchaidí.
I went backpacking on the Continent for a year in the '90s.

We didn't even use 'Europe' in Ireland back in the day. In households all across Ireland, it was always 'the Continent'. An Mhór-Roinn *sounds far away and warm, the perfect place to go interrailing.*

11 LÚNASA / 11 AUGUST

Caonach
Moss

[kway-nokh]

Bíonn an gairdín lán le caonach théis an gheimhridh fhliuch.
The garden is full of moss after the wet winter.

We have to be one of the best moss-growing countries in the world. It's on our trees, on our rocks, on our lawns and in the mountains. When you go into a moss-covered forest, it feels like it's been there for a long time. Caonach *thrives in our Irish ecosystem.*

12 LÚNASA / 12 AUGUST

Daidí na gcos fada
Daddy-long-legs

[daddy na guss faw-da]

Tagann daidí na gcos fada ag tús an tsamhraidh gach bliain.
Daddy-long-legs appear at the start of the summer every year.

I've come up with this word because I'm on a crusade with the *daidí na gcos fada*. I don't even want to know if there's a technical name for it. I've been fascinated by them since I was a child and I've always been trying to mind them, so now I want to save every one of them that lands in my house. At least three or four times a week during the summer, on those balmy evenings when the bathroom window is wide open, they end up on the inside of the window.

A daddy-long-legs doesn't mind you sneaking up on him – he probably knows that he needs help – so if I see one in the corner of the window, I will pick him up with the gentlest caress of one of his gangly legs. Then I lift him up to the open window and he flies off. Nobody knows what the job of a *daidí na gcos fada* is, but I make sure he gets back outside to do it.

What a great name for an insect, so I had to give it to you in Irish as well.

13 LÚNASA / 13 AUGUST

Cladach
Shoreline

[kla-dokh]

Bhí an currach thíos ag an gcladach i Leitir Móir.
The currach was down at the shoreline in Leitir Móir.

This is the purest of pure Connemara words. It has been enshrined in songs and ballads through the years. You will probably already know the word *trá*, but that's for the big beaches of the country like Bundoran and Bettystown – Tramore in Waterford is literally 'Big Beach'. *Cladach* is the word you need for those unspoiled little inlets and shorelines that are dotted around Connemara. They're the places you come across and say, 'Stop the car! Stop the car!' so you can get out and explore it. There are hundreds of these beautiful shorelines around, but when you come across one, you feel like Marco Polo, like you're the only person to have stepped foot on its soft, golden sand and for at least a couple of minutes you can think, 'This is mine'. Sometimes they're only 50 yards across; there might just be enough space to pull your fishing boat up on the shore.

These little inlets were formed over time by the ocean, carved into the nooks and crannies of Ireland, and *cladach* was carved into the Irish language to describe them.

14 LÚNASA / 14 AUGUST

Nead
Nest

[nyad]

Bhí nead déanta ag an éan sa chrann ar chúl an ghairdín.
A bird made a nest in the tree at the back of the garden.

15 LÚNASA / 15 AUGUST

Sinsir
Senior

[sheen-shur]

Tá craobh shinsir an chontae ar siúl an Domhnach seo chugainn.
The senior county final is on next Sunday.

Whenever I hear the word *sinsir* I think of all those great All-Ireland Finals of the 1960s and '70s and Mícheál O'Hehir saying, 'AND HERE COME THE SENIORS OF OFFALY!' Then all these men run out of the tunnel in their long shorts with their puffed-out chests, and there's a hundred thousand people in the stands, men in suits with big hair all swaying and smoking, ready to watch the soldiers of Croke Park play the game of a lifetime. The beautiful, passionate commentary of Mícheál O'Hehir is the soundtrack to these mighty battles, and when he says *sinsir*, well God almighty ... if it doesn't give you goosebumps, then nothing will.

Because that's the big question in Ireland: 'Do you play senior?' It's the be-all and end-all in any GAA club. For a child to go through their club from the under-8s, under-10s, under-12s and eventually play senior? It's a proud moment and the pinnacle of any young person's sporting career to say they play *sinsir* for their club and county.

16 LÚNASA / 16 AUGUST

Ar an imeall
On the edge

[air on imm-il]

Tá Gaillimh ar imeall na hEorpa.
Galway lies on the edge of Europe.

Ar an imeall *feels distant; it's almost like you're on the edge of the world. You can use it for far geographical reaches, when you reach the edge of a cliff and there is nowhere to go except down or if you are on the edge of a discovery, when you're pushing boundaries, almost falling off – but just clinging on.*

17 LÚNASA / 17 AUGUST

Matáin
Muscles

[matawn]

Bíonn matáin go leor sa gym áitúil.
There's plenty of muscles in the local gym.

My brother Freddie trained every day in the gym for about 30 years. I remember him leaving the house with a plastic bag and my mother said to him, 'Where are you going?' And when he said the gym, I said, 'What? Where the feck is the gym?' It was the first I'd heard of it. Freddie skedaddled off down the road in a U2 T-shirt with the sleeves cut off while me and my mother watched him out of the window of the kitchen extension. Mam said, 'What in the name of God is going on?' 'I don't know, Mam. I didn't even know there was a gym in Navan,' I replied.

That was about 1988, and since that day the gym became Freddie's life. He travelled to famous gyms around the world to train, the likes of Dorian Yates' gym in Birmingham and a place called Mjolnir in Reykjavik. Name a city in the world, and Freddie knew the best gym in it. He was so strong and ripped. I didn't know we had triceps in our family until I saw Freddie's. But then he showed me the way. Every time I saw him, he said I needed to go to a place called Galway City Gym, but I always thought, 'No way am I going to go.' But he managed to convince me, and it changed my life. I was never so proud as when I was able to WhatsApp Freddie a photo of my triceps. I had *matáin* of my own.

18 LÚNASA / 18 AUGUST

Seal a chaitheamh
To spend a while

[shall a ka-hiv]

Chaith mé seal thíos i Leacht Uí Chonchubhair an samhradh seo caite.
I spent a while down in Lahinch last summer.

When you really need to take a break and you decide to spend time with the kids or your partner or yourself, you can use seal a chaitheamh. *It's a time to repair yourself, maybe spend a while in the garden to recharge. It's not for long; it's just for a short time.*

19 LÚNASA / 19 AUGUST

Déagóirí
Teenagers

[day-gore-ee]

Bhí dioscó áitiúil ar siúl le haghaidh na ndéagóirí aréir.
The local teenage disco was on last night.

The teenage years are busy years. They're busy for Mam and Dad, and they're busy for the teenagers. It's out the door, in the door, schoolbag on the ground, out the door, football, back in the door, gear bag on the ground, dinner, sleep … 'I've a match tomorrow. Who's gonna bring me?' 'Where's my gumshield?' 'What's for dinner?' 'Where's my school blazer?' National school felt slow, peaceful, but secondary school went in the blink of an eye for us.

The teenage years are when the hugs go down in number, but the conversations go up. You walk into the kitchen and it's great to see those chats happening, and your teenagers knowing that there's love there. My youngest is 19 and at the end of it, and he's doing all the things 19-year-olds should be doing. He's driving, working away, playing Senior, and as I write this there's only a few months left until he's 20. We will soon have journeyed through the river rapids in the Gorge of the Teens and no longer have any *déagóirí* in our house.

20 LÚNASA / 20 AUGUST

Buaicphointí
Highlights

[boo-akh-fwin-tee]

Is breá liom na buaicphointí ar Match of the Day *oíche Dé Sathairn.*
I love the highlights on Match of the Day on Saturday nights.

Deh deh deh DEH de-deh deh deh dehhhh, deh dehhh de-deh deh DEHHHH ... When you hear the Match of the Day theme tune, you know exactly where you are and what time it is. Just like the Angelus at six o'clock or the nine o'clock news on RTÉ, these tunes are timepieces. They give you a sense of location. It's Saturday night and you're lying on the couch, ready to watch the soccer *buaicphointí*.

It was a big thing in our house. Our dad would break out the Morphy Richards sandwich toaster and the Soda Stream and we'd have our triangular ham-and-cheese toasties and flavoured fizzy water while we watched John Motson in his sheepskin jacket deliver the commentary from his massive microphone in the gantries of great British stadiums directly to our living room. And it wasn't just Man Utd and Liverpool; it was Ipswich Town and Nottingham Forest and Stoke City. We loved it all.

Match of the Day is a relic of the glory days when you followed soccer vigorously, before Sky and ESPN and satellite TV, but it's still the greatest soccer *buaicphointí* show of all time. And you have to hand it to the BBC: they know their theme tunes.

21 LÚNASA / 21 AUGUST

Soithí
Delph/dishes

[suh-hee]

Sa Ghaeltacht, bhí orainn na soithí a ní théis gach béile.
In the Gaeltacht, we had to do the dishes after every meal.

When dinner was over in the Gaeltacht, it was all hands on deck to clean up after. One lad would clear the table, someone else would be washing up, another would be drying and then there would be someone to put it away so everything would be ready again for supper the next day. I started this from the age of eight or nine, and it stood to me later in life. I love doing the delph now. There's something cathartic about squirting a load of Fairy Liquid into the sink to wash the *soithí* with someone standing beside you holding a tea towel that they've had to dig out of the big drawer of tea towels. It's the conveyor belt of Irish kitchens.

We always called it 'delph' in our house, which in itself is an interesting word. It's uniquely Irish to call the dishes 'delph'; they don't use it anywhere else in the world. So when you *nigh na soithí* in Irish, you 'wash the delph' in Hiberno-English.

22 LÚNASA / 22 AUGUST

Beart
Parcel

[bart]

Fuair mé beart sa phost ar maidin.
I got a parcel in the post this morning.

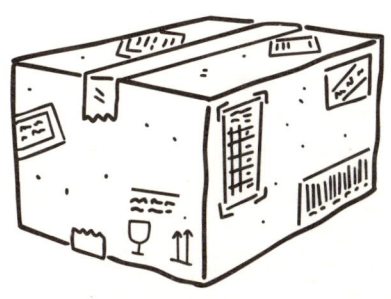

23 LÚNASA / 23 AUGUST

Mo mhuintir
My people

[muh ween-ter]

Is as Contaetha na Mí agus na Gaillimhe mo mhuintir.
My people come from Meath and Galway.

Your people are your extended family, your tribal family. You share the same name, but you might not be related. I recently found out that there are a load of Keogans in New Zealand. They left Ireland during the Famine and fled to the South Island. The Keogans aren't a massive clan, but I do bump into one the odd time when I'm out and about. I was at a concert with Dympna and my two boys years ago in Pearse Stadium in Galway, and we were in the little chipboard area in the gantry. I look over and who's beside me, only Barry Keoghan. It was around 2018 and his star was on the rise. He said, 'How's it going, Hector?' and we got chatting. I told him, 'Do you know my surname in English is your surname?' and he went, 'No fucking way!' in that Dublin accent. I said, 'Right, I'm going to give you your name in Irish now.' He took out his phone and wrote it down, and when I've bumped into him a couple of times since, he always laughs and says, 'Barry Ó hEochagáin'.

Donal Keogan is a legendary footballer from Meath, and I met another one of my people in Shanette Sheds in Kilbeggan when I was buying a shed. I walked into the showroom and when the boss came out, I knew from the way he talked that he was one of my people, and then he said, 'I'm a Keogan too.' He even had ginger hair and a pasty face.

There might not be many Keogans, but *mo mhuintir* stretches from shed shops in the midlands of Ireland to New Zealand and Hollywood.

24 LÚNASA / 24 AUGUST

Neamhspleách
Independent

[nyav-splokh]

Rith sí mar iarrthóir neamhspleách sa toghcán an bhliain seo caite.
She ran as an independent candidate in last year's election.

I like to think that I've always been an independent person. I had to learn to look after myself quickly when I moved out of home at 17 to go to university in Dublin. Survival and independence go hand in hand. When you learn to survive and get on in life, you gain a level of independence. Back then, before the accommodation shortage and astronomical rents, so many people left their family homes to go to college in another city, and independence came part and parcel with the degree.

Being independent is a talent; it's a trait that should be encouraged and nurtured, but I don't think it can be taught. It's a great thing to be able to do things on your own, to find a job and a place to live and even get your own car. But that's all much harder to do now than it was when I went to college, and to solve that problem we need *neamhspleách* thinkers.

25 LÚNASA / 25 AUGUST

Ceathrú
Quarter

[kah-roo]

– *Cén t-am é?*
– *Tá sé ceathrú chun a trí.*
– What time is it?
– It's a quarter to three.

This is an essential word for telling time in Irish. In Ireland, things either start at a quarter past or a quarter to – there's no other time that matters. 'What time is kick off?' 'Ceathrú tar éis a trí.'

26 LÚNASA / 26 AUGUST

Fásach
Desert

[faw-sokh]

Bhí mé i bhFásach an tSahára an tseachtain seo caite.
I was in the Sahara Desert last week.

I'll never forget the first time I got to the Sahara Desert. To me, it was the pinnacle of my travels, to leave from Cairo with a load of Bedouin and nomad lads. We were heading out about 500 kilometres in a convoy of jeeps to the White Desert, which is known for its mushroom-like dunes.

After about a seven- or eight-hour journey, we found a place to camp for the night. And I'll never forget these Bedouin boys pulling their stuff out of the back of the jeeps and creating this amazing miniature campsite, with lovely multicoloured blankets everywhere. It was like everything I'd seen on *Sinbad* growing up. Me, Rosco and Evan all wanted to get in touch with home to let them know we were alright, but we had no coverage on our mobile phones. One of the lads noticed and walked us up the side of a big sand dune, with nothing but the light of the stars above us, and told us to point our phones that way – towards Cairo. Then I was able to text Dympna and say, 'Everything is okay. I love you.'

The Sahara is the rooftop of Africa, and I was enchanted by it. I fell in love with the dunes and the Tuareg tribes and the music – I still listen to Tinariwen; they're like the Jimi Hendrix Experience of the desert. I was out in the middle of the Sahara with a load of Bedouins, and all I wanted to do was walk away from the tents barefooted up the side of the sand dunes and into the *fásach* that went on forever.

27 LÚNASA / 27 AUGUST

Cosantóir
Defender

[kus-an-tore]

Ba é Martin O'Connell ó Chontae na Mí ceann de na cosantóirí ab fhearr riamh sa CLG.
Martin O'Connell from Meath was one of the greatest defenders of all time in the GAA.

Everybody needs a good cosantóir *on their team, everybody needs someone to defend them in life and everybody likes looking at a Defender jeep.*

28 LÚNASA / 28 AUGUST

Líon damháin alla
Spiderweb

[lee-un dow-awn a-la]

Bhí líon damháin alla thuas ar an síleáil sa seomra folctha.
There was a spider's web up on the ceiling in the bathroom.

29 LÚNASA / 29 AUGUST

Lúibíní
Brackets

[loo-been-ee]

Níor úsáid mé lúibíní ó bhí mé sa mheánscoil.
I haven't used brackets since I was in secondary school.

Even though I wasn't a swot in Irish, I learned the word lúibíní*. I used to love putting them in my essays in secondary school, but I rarely use them these days. I don't know how many editors or writers will be reading this book, but this one's for you.*

30 LÚNASA / 30 AUGUST

An tslí
The way

[on tslee]

Bhí an tslí ar fad isteach go dtí an sráidbhaile faoi uisce.
The whole way into the village was under water.

In a depiction of an Irish valley, the forest trail going off into the distance epitomises what an tslí *is, or the path in the garden the dog has carved out. We need to know our way to town and our way through life.*

31 LÚNASA / 31 AUGUST

Iasacht
Loan

[ee-as-okht]

Fuair mé iasacht airgid ó chara maith liom.
I got a loan of money from a good friend.

When I was living in Killiney in Dublin, my mates from Navan would stay over in the house after a night out. One of those mates was Steven Deegan. He worked for his dad delivering hair products in bulk to hair salons. I used to go with him in the van to check out the talent – those hairdressers were gorgeous to two young lads flying around in a HiAce.

One of the days out on his deliveries, Steven hit another vehicle. It was a posh southside Dublin car, like a Jaguar. To avoid his father finding out about the accident, he offered to get the dent fixed and paint job done as soon as possible. The Jaguar driver agreed. The problem was that he needed 750 quid, and quick. He called up to me in Killiney to ask for a loan, and luckily I had two grand saved in the Irish Permanent. Steven got the car fixed in Dublin and his father was none the wiser.

About three months later, on a night out in The International Bar in Dublin with a clatter of pints taken, Steven gave me an envelope with 750 quid in it. I woke up the next day hungover, and I couldn't find the envelope. I searched upstairs, downstairs, jeans pockets, jacket pockets. I retraced my steps back to The International, up the stairs to where we were sitting, then to the manky huge pub dustbins ... nothing. Where the hell was the envelope? The search continued all week until I resigned myself to losing it. 'You eejit!' I thought. '750 quid cash gone.'

Six months later, we were moving out of the house in Killiney. I was cleaning out my bedroom when I moved the entire bedframe out from the wall, and there under the mattress was an envelope full of fifty-pound notes. The 750 quid *iasacht* I gave Steven had been there all along.

1 MEÁN FÓMHAIR / 1 SEPTEMBER

Tost
Silence

[tust]

Thit an teach tábhairne ina thost nuair a chan sé an t-amhrán.
The pub fell silent when he sang the song.

It's a special moment, almost a spiritual one, and it doesn't happen all the time. But when it does, it's special – that sense of enthralment that can bring about silence. It's something we have all experienced, and it happens in the Irish pub.

The cold winter's night, the fire burning in the corner, the hissing of the Guinness tap in full flow, the crowd adin ('adin' is Meath for 'inside'), the chatter and laughter throughout the bar, tunes flowing in the session in the corner. Then, all of a sudden, a voice picks up a note and the song begins. And if the voice is good and the song is the right one, a still, respectful silence descends, and the crowd that had just been chattering and laughing fall into a hush and let the song drift over them. Even the barman stops his work and places his hand on top of the Guinness tap to listen. This type of singer might only sing once a year; it might be the rare time that they perform a ballad that can command the attention of a noisy crowd in your local pub with one soft note. It's amazing how the power of a single voice can do that. It's so nice to slow down, be *in do thost*, and tune in to the magic of a beautiful voice.

2 MEÁN FÓMHAIR / 2 SEPTEMBER

Fíniúin
Vine

[feen-oo-in]

Bhí an fhíniúin lán de thorthaí.
The vine was full of fruit.

Vine, the Equaliser
2 SEPTEMBER–29 SEPTEMBER

If you were born around this time of year, the Celtic tree of your birth is the vine. I'm told vine people are great diplomats. They love to hammer things out and get things sorted.

But apart from the tomatoes some of us manage to grow in little greenhouses out the back, Irish eyes don't really know what vines look like. We are turnip and spud people, carrot and parsnip heads. Our land is rich, but it doesn't give us vines.

The most remarkable vines I've ever seen happen to be in New Zealand, in a place near the Bay of Plenty on the North Island. This is where the juiciest kiwis on the planet grow. Never before have I seen such abundance of produce growing in front of my eyes. This is the La Rioja of New Zealand, but instead of grapes there are kiwis.

As we drove into the farm, there were kiwi vines as far as the eye could see, field after field on gentle slopes. With kiwis, the central vines are tied in strands of four like a tepee, so all around were these amazing pyramid-like structures laden with fruit. Nothing can prepare your brain for the moment you crouch down and head under the canopy into the orchards. Millions of the ripest, most golden kiwis hung five or six per vine. The vine had done its job and it was a bumper harvest. I picked one from the *fíniúin* and munched deep ... *stop na soilse!* (Stop the lights!)

3 MEÁN FÓMHAIR / 3 SEPTEMBER

Duilleog
Leaf

[dill-owg]

Thosaigh na duilleoga ag titim.
The leaves started to fall.

4 MEÁN FÓMHAIR / 4 SEPTEMBER

Snag breac
Magpie

[snawg brack]

Tá nead snag breac sa pháirc taobh thiar de mo theach.
There's a magpie nest in the field at the back of my house.

There was a time there when I was fierce superstitious, especially when it came to the magpies. Now when I look back on it, it was around the time my mother, Trina, died suddenly, and you sort of think about everything in those weeks and month – even years – that follow. It's hard to say whether the superstition was related, but I do know I was daydreaming a lot, even while driving the car. My mind was there on the road, but it was also away somewhere else. And if you threw in a magpie along the road, then away I went. 'Shite, where's the next one? Not sorrow ... not more sorrow, gimme joy. Where the hell is the other magpie?' One for sorrow, two for joy, three for a girl, four for a boy ... Surely it's only an aul wives' tale, isn't it? But I'd be thinking about my mother and then I'd see a magpie.

After about a year or so, I realised there was a nest of magpies in a hedge quite close to the house, a full family of them. A group of magpies can be called a 'mischief' or a 'charm'. Either way, they're unique aul birds. They come from the crow dynasty, and God knows we have some of the biggest, most powerful crows on the planet in Ireland. But even those powerful crows skedaddle when the *snaganna breaca* are in town. And for me, as time has gone on, I don't worry about them any more.

5 MEÁN FÓMHAIR / 5 SEPTEMBER

Cromán; Crománach
Hip; Hipster

[crum-awn; crum-awn-okh]

Fuair m'uncail cromán nua an bhliain seo caite.
My uncle got a new hip last year.
Bíonn croiméil ar na crománaigh na laethanta seo.
The hipsters are all into the moustaches these days.

I want to give a shout-out to all the people who just got the hip replaced. It must be one of the great Irish operations. If your mother or father or aunt or uncle have to go into hospital, you know it's to get the hip done. I think we're the hip-replacement capital of the world. It's because they were jiving for 20 years. I blame Dickie Rock and all the showbands for breaking the hips of our parents or grandparents on the dance floors of their youths.

I want you to sit back now and think of how many members of your family have had their hip done. And now I want you to think of how many hipsters you know, because I've invented a new word in the Irish language: *crománach*. I took the word for 'hip' and created the word for 'hipster', because it's not in the Irish–English dictionary. I filmed a series all over Australia for TG4 in 2025, and there's an Aussie hipster look that is rapidly taking over the Western world. It's the mullet haircut with the short moustache that's been exported from Perth to Portlaoise. I want you all to start using *crománach* to help it to catch on and be officially recognised. Let's use it often, so I can get a word of my own invention in the dictionary. Up the *cromán* replacements and up the *crománach*!

6 MEÁN FÓMHAIR / 6 SEPTEMBER

Lár na páirce
Midfield

[lore na porka]

Tá imreoir speisialta ag teastáil i lár na páirce na laethanta seo, ar nós Brian Fenton ó Bhaile Átha Cliath.
There's a special type of player needed these days at midfield, like Brian Fenton from Dublin.

This literally means 'middle of the park'. They're the heroes in the middle, the likes of Mick O'Connell, Dermot Earley Senior, Brian Mullins, Jack O'Shea, Gerry McEntee, Liam Hayes, James McCarthy, Brian Fenton and Paul Conroy. Then there's the lads with the sticks in their hands: John Fenton, Frank Cummins, Michael Fennelly, Tony Browne, Cian Lynch, David Burke. There are too many to mention, but they're all mountains of men *i lár na páirce*.

7 MEÁN FÓMHAIR / 7 SEPTEMBER

In aon chor
At all, whatsoever

[in ain kor]

Bhí an traein plódaithe; ní raibh aon spás ann in aon chor.
The train was packed; there was no space whatsoever.

This a lovely one to use when you know you can't make the wedding date, when you know you can't go out because you have work the next morning, when you know that there's not a hope in hell of you getting off the couch, because that's just the way it is. And the addition of in aon chor *at the end shows you really mean it.*

8 MEÁN FÓMHAIR / 8 SEPTEMBER

Aireagán
Invention

[arr-a-gawn]

Is aireagán iontach é an teileafón.
The telephone is a great invention.

Anyone who invents something has to be applauded and lauded. It's an incredible thing to visualise, plan and build an idea into reality. If you remember *coincheap* (brainwave) from 8 March, you'll know I love a good firelog, but my favourite invention has to be the ride-on lawnmower. I love my ride-on as much as I love my car. It even has a winter coat. I cover the engine with old coats and blankets to keep it warm over the winter months, and I start it on frosty days to make sure it's alright. If you don't care for your ride-on in the winter, your ride-on won't care for you in the summer.

The ride-on resides in the shed and is there all the time just waiting for me. I even sort of hide the keys to the shed, because it's *my* shed. Then when April comes, the weather is beautiful and the ground is dry, and you're ready for the first cut of the year, so you make the pilgrimage to the garden shed. Then I give the ride-on a little bit of the clutch and a little bit of the choke and *vroom*, I'm off! To me, one of the great moments in your life is when you're up the garden on your ride-on lawnmower.

My mother won a Mountfield Briggs & Stratton ride-on lawnmower in the school raffle in 1979 and it revolutionised our garden. Me and my brothers used to fight over who would get to cut the lawn, all because it had a lever with a hare on it to go fast and a lever with a tortoise on it to go slow. I think that's where my love of ride-on lawnmowers started. Whoever decided to put a saddle and big wheels on a lawnmower is a genius. It really is the best *aireagán* ever.

9 MEÁN FÓMHAIR / 9 SEPTEMBER

Machnamh
Thought, contemplation

[mock-nuv]

Caithfidh mé machnamh a dhéanamh air.
I'll have to think about it.

Machnamh *is a beautiful-sounding word, but you have to say it slowly. It's for when you have to go away and really think about something. It's the 'can we go to the back of the room and talk' moment on* Dragon's Den. Machnamh *means careful consideration.*

10 MEÁN FÓMHAIR / 10 SEPTEMBER

Diallait
Saddle

[dee-a-lit]

Ba é Paul Carberry an leaid ab fhearr sa diallait a chonaic mé riamh.
Paul Carberry was the best man in the saddle that I've ever seen.

I used to own a horse. He was called Steve Capall after the great Man Utd player Steve Coppell of the 1970s and early '80s ... and, of course, after 'horse' in Irish. He was a really good horse; not a lot of them are. I bought a leg of him while playing a game of squash in NUIG. Not sure if I won the game, but I left the court with a stake in a racehorse. The lads who owned the rest of him owned bars in Galway, including the Róisín Dubh. I knew they had horses and I knew they had winners, and you need to be in with lucky lads when you buy a share in a horse.

Our horse won its first race, a bumper in Thurles with the great Nina Carberry in the saddle. We were as high as kites. A few weeks later, Steve Capall went over hurdles and won again – this time in Kilbeggan, the sleepy little backwater racecourse of the midlands. We were higher than kites.

The Galway races were coming up and it's the be-all and end-all of the racing calendar for most – it's seven days in July and it's party central for the city. And Steve won again, this time with Paul Carberry in the *diallait*. Thinking I couldn't get a higher buzz, I did ... I led him into the ring and it was live on TG4. I can't remember much after that; as I said, the lads owned pubs!

11 MEÁN FÓMHAIR / 11 SEPTEMBER

Cliobóg
Leapfrog

[klib-owg]

Bhí na páistí ag imirt cliobóige sa chlós.
The children were playing leapfrog in the yard.

You only play leapfrog with your pals between the ages of five and ten, and then you don't think of it again. It's a game for schoolyards, and cliobóg *is a great word for national school teachers to have.*

12 MEÁN FÓMHAIR / 12 SEPTEMBER

Castán
Chestnut

[kos-tawn]

Bhí an buachaill óg ag bailiú castán.
The young boy was collecting chestnuts.

I can't tell you how important chestnuts were to me as a child. The beauty of seeing the green spiky balls on the ground, splitting one open and seeing the gorgeous shiny chestnut in the centre. Playing conkers was a big part of my childhood. The key was to find a nice big one and let it dry out on the windowsill. Then you would go out to the garage to get a hammer and drive a big nail through it. The laces for my shoes were often taken out to be attached to the conkers. Sometimes I'd even go down to the local cobbler to buy a new pack of laces. Then you would bring a few into school to play at break and it was just magnificent.

Playing conkers should be an Olympic sport. There's a World Conker Championship every year, and no doubt there are heats in Ireland to qualify. But I can guarantee you it would never match the satisfaction of playing conkers in the yard in national school with your pals. And I know, come September, I'll still see kids out looking for the perfect *castán*.

13 MEÁN FÓMHAIR / 13 SEPTEMBER

Deis
Opportunity

[desh]

Thug an Ghaeilge deis dom taisteal ar fud an domhain.
Irish has given me the opportunity to travel all over the world.

Deis is a lovely way of saying you were given a chance to do something. It's almost like a door opened for you, and you were given the opportunity to go somewhere or study at college or do something new. Everyone needs an opportunity at some point in their life. It's like we say in Ireland, 'Who gave you the start?' Maybe you got the start working for the summer in Boston or doing a few shifts for your friend in the local factory.

The Irish language handed me a *deis* when I was offered a job in TG4, and I'm glad I took it. An opportunity is a chance to move forward, broaden your horizons, have new experiences, so we should always be ready to say yes to the *deis*. Grab it with both hands, because you never know where it will lead you.

14 MEÁN FÓMHAIR / 14 SEPTEMBER

Diúilicín
Mussel

[due-luh-keen]

Bhí me thíos ag an trá sa Cheathrú Rua agus bhí sé lán de dhiúilicíní.
I was down at the beach in Carraroe and it was full of mussels.

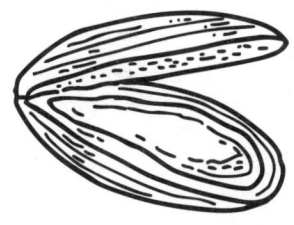

15 MEÁN FÓMHAIR / 15 SEPTEMBER

Culaith scoile
School uniform

[kull-a skull-ya]

Cá bhfuil do chulaith scoile?
Where's your school uniform?

We've had some craic with our boys' uniforms over the years in this house. The school uniform in national school is quite easy, because you're able to locate it after they take it off. But once you get into secondary school, you enter the horror show. On Sunday night it's, 'Where's your pants and jumper?' Walking out the door on Monday morning it's, 'Where's your tie?' And that's the way it was, all the way from first year to sixth year. I think Oppenheimer had an easier job making the nuclear bomb than parents trying to get two teenagers out of bed and into their uniforms at twenty to eight on a Monday morning.

And you know they will be reprimanded in school if they don't have their blazers, because the school is very picky about uniforms. It would drive me mental. They have the big woolly jumper on, designed for the middle of winter, and they have to wear the blazer over it even when the sun is bating through the window. They had to have their initials embroidered on the blazer and that didn't make a difference at all. There were blazers of lads I'd never heard of in my house. I'd be going, 'Who the hell is Keith Gillespie? What are you doing in a first year's blazer when you're in fifth year?' It didn't even fit him, but he'd wear it just to get in the door of the school.

You look at photos of them on their first day in secondary school and they look pristine, and then at the end of sixth year the uniform is unrecognisable. I was never so happy to get rid of that blazer when my youngest finished secondary school. It was the bane of our lives. I wanted to make a funeral pyre out the back to burn the whole *culaith scoile*.

16 MEÁN FÓMHAIR / 16 SEPTEMBER

Gealach na gcoinlíní
Harvest moon

[gyal-okh na gwin-lee-nee]

Níl rud ar bith níos deise ná gealach na gcoinlíní i Meán Fómhair.
There's nothing more beautiful than the harvest moon in September.

The harvest moon always makes me think of the Neil Young song. I used to fall asleep listening to a Neil Young compilation when I lived in the Basque Country, around 1993 or '94. We would be having a great time, possibly even having partaken of the finest pollen from Morocco, and at the end of every night I would put on music in my apartment. I can hear the opening line in my head as I write this. 'Harvest Moon' will always make me think of those times in Bilbao, and a *gealach na gcoinlíní* will always stop me in my tracks. It looks almost supernatural, just sitting at the end of the road as you stroll home. You expect E.T. to fly across it on a high nelly bicycle.

You might be on your way back from a long day at work or volunteering in the local club, the kids in the back of the car, and all that's on your mind is what you're going to make for dinner – but if you see a harvest moon, you have to stop the car and get out to admire what Mother Nature has put in front of you. A big light in the sky to guide you home.

17 MEÁN FÓMHAIR / 17 SEPTEMBER

Leite
Porridge

[letcha]

Is aoibhinn liom leite do mo bhricfeasta ar mhaidin fhuar.
I love porridge for breakfast on a cold morning.

We were never porridge people in our house. We were consumers of the UK-based cereals: the likes of Weetabix, Rice Krispies, Shredded Wheat. Even though my mother never gave me porridge, she did give me a version of porridge that fell into the 'UK-based cereals' category: Ready Brek. The classic breakfast before you stick on your duffle coat and walk to school for 20 miles with a glowing red tummy.

Now I've gone through phases of having porridge for breakfast as an adult. We've done the blueberries and honey on top and the overnight oats, but to me there's still something a bit *Oliver* about a bowl of porridge – it's a cousin of gruel. So we wouldn't be big porridge heads, but a few times a year we'll dip out of the UK-based cereals and back into the porridge, so we'll pick up our bag of Flahavan's in the supermarket. A shout-out to Mary Flahavan and John Flahavan and their people for putting breakfast on the tables of Ireland for generations. They're one of the great Irish companies that have lasted. I met them once and learned loads about how they make the oats. They use the same river to power the mill and the same techniques now as they did when your granny was eating *leite* for breakfast.

18 MEÁN FÓMHAIR / 18 SEPTEMBER

Orlach
Inch

[ur-lok]

Tá sé orlach déag ar an rialóir adhmaid a bhí againn ar scoil.
The wooden ruler we used to have at school is 16 inches long.

I'm in awe of people who can use measuring tapes because I'm terrible with measurements. I have no more idea what a centimetre looks like than I do an orlach. *The only thing in the house I know the measurement of in inches is the plasma screen.*

19 MEÁN FÓMHAIR / 19 SEPTEMBER

Crannchur
Raffle

[kron-khur]

Ar chuala tú gur bhuaigh Fidelma carr sa chrannchur?
Did you hear Fidelma won a car in the raffle?

I get asked to do fundraisers all the time. It happens when you're sort of well known in a small parish. 'Hector, we're doing *The Cube* for charity down the hall. Will you host?' And if you host the night in any GAA institution, there's always a raffle. The committee have been working away to get all the raffle books together and about 50 prizes that range from a night away in a nice hotel to a tin of USA biscuits. And I can guarantee you, the draw never takes place before midnight. Everyone is half sloshed, so they don't know if they're looking at the cream ticket or the yellow ticket. It's an absolute raffle minefield. By the time we get to prize number 40, if I'm looking for a green ticket and they hold up a blue ticket, I'll just say, 'Yeah, that's it' to keep things moving. People love buying strips and strips of tickets, and raffles are a great way to make money for a local club or charity.

I like doing the odd *crannchur* myself. When we're away filming the travel show and we pull up in a small town, me and Rosco and Evan will go into the petrol station and buy a ticket for the local lotto. We do it for the craic and to get rid of the boredom after spending 14 hours in a HiAce van. There must be something in our Irish blood that makes us love a *crannchur* enough to buy a ticket in the middle of nowhere in Australia.

20 MEÁN FÓMHAIR / 20 SEPTEMBER

Ag druidim le
Nearing, approaching

[egg drih-jim leh]

Bhíomar ag druidim leis an gcathair le titim na hoíche.
We were getting close to the city as night fell.

One of my favourite words of all time. I love the sound of it, the feel of it, the significance of it. This is for when the days are getting shorter or that feeling of a long journey coming to an end as you near your destination ...

21 MEÁN FÓMHAIR / 21 SEPTEMBER

Fan amach ó
Stay well away from

[fan am-ok oh]

Fan orm
Wait for me
Fan liomsa
Stay with me

The triple fan *... what a powerful little word. It has so many uses, all depending on the structure when used and the loudness of the voice behind it. The first one is the angry dad telling the 14-year-old off for something that happened at school, to stay away from the bad influence. The second is rushing for the train along the platform and your best friend gets ahead of you. And the third* fan *is the offer of a bed to rest your head after a night out that you didn't plan.*

22 MEÁN FÓMHAIR / 22 SEPTEMBER

Feadóg
Whistle

[fad-owg]

Shéid an réiteoir an fheadóg: bhí an t-am istigh.
The referee blew the whistle: time was up.

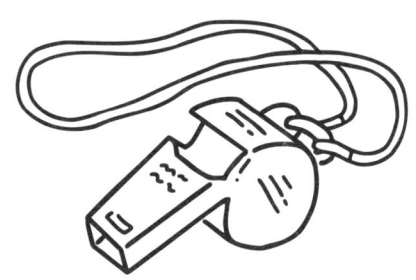

23 MEÁN FÓMHAIR / 23 SEPTEMBER

Bonn
Medal

[baun]

Bhuaigh mé bonn óir inné ag an lá spóirt.
I won a gold medal at sports day yesterday.

The mother's house in Navan is full of medals. There was a time when me and the brothers were all doing athletics – 100 metres, 400 metres, relays – it was a jamboree of running events. We were part of the South O'Hanlon Club, and we trained in a small meadow-type field on the Kells Road, just past the train tracks. The grass in the middle of the meadow was cut in a large circle to make the 100-metre sprint track, and we had a small old prefab as a changing room. It was basic, but it was brilliant.

In winter we ran cross-country in our dark maroon singlets, through gaps in hedges, over ditches and streams and across open fields (and this was long before the likes of Hell & Back). We did races all over the country, and one of my best memories was when I finished fourth in the under-12s 100-metre national finals of the Community Games at Mosney. I had a really bad start and I just missed out by a head on a bronze medal to a lad from Tipperary.

Many years later, I interviewed Carl Lewis in a dugout at a university in Texas, where he's in charge of a load of athletes and about a $25 million budget. So I sit there and I tell one of the greatest sprinters of all time, who has ten Olympic *boinn*, nine of them gold, that I used to be a sprinter myself. He listened politely while I said, 'I finished fourth in the under-12s finals at the Community Games. And it was only by a pip; I got a bad start,' and he said, 'Wow, that's awesome, the Community Games. I've never heard of those.' I doubt he's ever been to Mosney either.

24 MEÁN FÓMHAIR / 24 SEPTEMBER

Teach ceann tuí
Thatched-roof house

[tyokh kyaun tee]

Tá teach ceann tuí in aice le teach mo mháthar san Uaimh.
There's a thatched-roof house beside my mother's house in Navan.

My daily route to school or town as a child growing up in Navan consisted of a walk past my grandmother's old thatched-roof cottage. It was whitewashed and surrounded by large conifers, fields and paddocks. It was pure countryside, yet so close to town. My father's family had a farmhouse with some sheds around it just up the way from the cottage. I can't picture them in my head any more – the memory has faded – but I can still see my grandmother's thatched cottage vividly in my mind's eye. In later years, no one lived in the cottage and the roof fell into disrepair, so sadly it disappeared.

In the village in Galway where I live now, there's a cottage that had its roof rethatched last year, and I was in awe of the skill and the artistry involved in it. I pulled in one day to chat to the couple who were doing it. They said they were flat to the mat with work, as the traditional thatched roof was making a bit of a comeback. It's nice hearing that sort of thing. If only that were the case back in the day, my grandmother's *teach ceann tuí* would still be there, on the bend on the country road on the way into town.

25 MEÁN FÓMHAIR / 25 SEPTEMBER

Buille
Smack, belt, wallop

[bwill-ya]

Fuair sé buille ceart sa chloigeann.
He got a right belt in the head.

We have a strong tendency to say someone got a 'right' bang on the head. The inclusion of the word 'right' gives it strength, almost like a kudos to the level of smack they got. Whether it's a child falling off a swing or two under-12s clashing heads going for the ball at a GAA match, 'Jesus Christ, he got a right *buille* there.'

26 MEÁN FÓMHAIR / 26 SEPTEMBER

Den scoth
Top notch

[den skuh]

Bhí béile den scoth againn aréir sa bhialann.
We had a top-notch meal last night in the restaurant.

Whether it's a tremendous pint of Guinness or a magnificent seafood chowder, a film where you sit through all the credits at the end or a book you simply can't put down, *den scoth* is the go-to phrase. If something is magnificent, superb, all the description you need is here in this phrase. It's universal and it always works, so it's a great one to add to your arsenal of Irish vocabulary.

When we get those surprise weeks of sunshine in April or September, we can say we had *aimsir den scoth* – top-notch weather, out of nowhere, that disappears as quickly as it appeared. *Den scoth* isn't a phrase that you would use all the time – but when you do, by God, people get exactly what you're talking about. It's the highest of praises.

27 MEÁN FÓMHAIR / 27 SEPTEMBER

Dlúthchara
Best friend

[dloo-ka-ra]

Tá mo dhlúthchara ag bogadh sall go Vancouver.
My best friend is moving over to Vancouver.

My first group of best friends were all from around Navan, and I would meet them every day at the top of the road beside the Moatville estate. We'd walk to school together every morning and play soccer every evening. But my childhood friends are not my best friends now. Playing together as kids was about football, but then playing together as adults was about going out for pints and to nightclubs. So your best friends change as you grow up.

I was a bit of a nomad, and I made new best friends wherever I moved: I collected them in Dublin, the Gaeltacht, Bilbao ... But then I relocated my whole life to Galway in the West of Ireland, and since then I've met all my best friends in the City of the Tribes.

Your *dlúthchairde* are the ones you're really tight with, the ones who have stuck around for 20 or 30 years. They're not necessarily down the road or even in the same city, but you're probably all in a WhatsApp group. You have to go through lots of mad and sad experiences together to be best friends. I had a great time in my 20s with the lads drinking flagons of cider and going to rock festivals, and now that we're older, we're tied together by those memories because that's where our friendship was forged. We'll get together a few times a year and it's like nothing has changed. If you have *dlúthchairde*, you should always mind them.

28 MEÁN FÓMHAIR / 28 SEPTEMBER

Corrán gealaí
Crescent moon

[kurr-awn gya-lee]

Bíonn corrán gealaí le feiceáil faoi dhó gach mí.
A crescent moon can be seen twice every month.

29 MEÁN FÓMHAIR / 29 SEPTEMBER

Bhailigh siad leo
Off they went

[wal-lee sheed low]

Phacáil siad na málaí agus bhailigh siad leo chuig an Astráil.
They packed their bags and off they went to Australia.

My mother, Trina, would say they 'skedaddled', and that's a perfect translation for this. It gives me an image in my head of a cowboy on his horse at the end of a Western, riding off into the sunset. It's for when your friends up sticks and move to Australia, or they do an Irish goodbye from the pub. One minute they're there, the next they're gone. Bailithe leo.

30 MEÁN FÓMHAIR / 30 SEPTEMBER

Eidhneán
Ivy

[eye-nawn]

Thar na blianta bhí an t-eidhneán ag fás ar chúl an tseantí.
Over the years the ivy grew at the back of the old house.

Ivy, the Survivor
30 SEPTEMBER–27 OCTOBER

If you were born between now and the end of October, ivy is your Celtic tree. You're well able to look after yourself, like ivy clinging to a garden fence. I lost a fence covered in *eidhneán* that had lasted 20 years in a big storm recently, and if you'd seen the way the roots were embedded in the ground and the vines clung to the fence – it was like a web of strength. What a symbol of power.

1 DEIREADH FÓMHAIR / 1 OCTOBER

Dorchadas
Darkness

[durr-a-kud-us]

Tá an geimhreadh ag teacht agus an dorchadas leis.
Winter is coming and the darkness with it.

I like October, and I don't mind it when the evenings get darker. I live in the countryside and there are no street lights, so the *dorchadas* is all around. I suppose I'm used to it. The only light is usually when we have a big, bright moon when the sky is clear. It's amazing how powerful it is. You can sometimes see your shadow on the laneways from the light it gives out. Once you have a bright moon or the torch on your phone – which is the best thing they ever decided to put on a mobile – the darkness is no problem.

The sky at night is completely different in Galway and Australia. Now that's true darkness. I spent time in the Bush with an Aboriginal astronomer and there's no light pollution there at all. We sat looking at the stars and he painted a picture for me of what Aboriginal people see when they look at the constellations. They see animals in the stars, connecting the sky with what they see around them in nature on the land.

It would be nice to do a bit of stargazing at home where I live in Galway, because there's so little light pollution, but the Atlantic dominates our sky. Whenever there's a chance to see an amazing star or the Northern Lights or something, nine times out of ten it will be cloudy.

2 DEIREADH FÓMHAIR / 2 OCTOBER

Ríomhaire
Computer

[reev-er-a]

Cheannaigh mé mo chéad ríomhaire in 2000.
I bought my first computer in 2000.

My computer education started with a Microsoft Word course from a FÁS scheme back around 1994. FÁS also paid for my driving lessons; it was brilliant. I can drive no problem, but I still type with my two index fingers.

Not too long after the course, I got my first job in television. I started working for a local production company in Galway called Magma Films. It was owned by a giant, gregarious German called Ralf who had fallen in love with the West of Ireland. He lived in a castle outside Galway and he made cartoons for the German market. He had bought a range of Apple Macs for the company, and I remember them clearly. The backs were covered in a translucent orange or blue or green so you could see all the wires, and when you turned them on they went, 'Ga-JOOOOOOONG!' I remember how cool I felt because I lived in Galway and I worked for a giant German who lived in a castle.

Getting a computer back then was like buying a car, so not many households had them. They were expensive and they were big. The backs of those Macs were the size of Volkswagen Beetles. I didn't get my own *ríomhaire* until the turn of the millennium, and by then they were more compact, but I'll never forget how much I loved those days sitting at my giant Mac at Magma Films.

3 DEIREADH FÓMHAIR / 3 OCTOBER

Dialann
Diary

[dee-a-lin]

Bhí dialann agam fadó nuair a bhí mé i mo dhéagóir.
I had a diary years ago as a teenager.

I didn't have a diary growing up. It was hard enough for me to keep up with the music on *Top of the Pops*, hanging out with the lads and trying to be cool. Even as I got older and started working as a freelancer, I didn't keep a diary. You'd think I'd need one to keep track of everything, but what would I be writing in a diary? 'Important meeting: Dublin' or 'Get Fairy Liquid and toilet paper'?

The heyday of diaries had to have been when the Filofax came out. They had the thin flippy pages and the little pen stuck to the side so you could write all your appointments in it. It was for busy executives and people who thought they were busy executives. I was the opposite of that.

I remember pitching the TV show *Only Fools Buy Horses* to a commissioning editor in RTÉ. I typed up the pitch for the show and went to a print shop in Galway to print it out, and it fitted on a single A4 sheet. I managed to get to Dublin on the train and out to Donnybrook without crumpling my one page. All that was on it was the name of the show, the style of the show, the tone of the show and the target audience. I pushed it across the table, gave the pitch out of my head, and managed to get a six-part series greenlit. I'm very proud of that, and I didn't miss a meeting even though I didn't have a *dialann* to write the dates in.

4 DEIREADH FÓMHAIR / 4 OCTOBER

Bróga reatha
Runners

[bro-ga ra-ha]

Cheannaigh mé péire bróg reatha inné le haghaidh an mharatóin.
I bought a pair of runners yesterday for the marathon.

Díograiseach
Dedicated

[dee-o-gras-okh]

Tá an chlann sin an-díograiseach faoin gclub áitiúil.
That family are really dedicated to the local club.

I like this word; it carries weight. It's a lovely thing to be díograiseach *to something or someone, to be dedicated to a cause, a movement, a passion or a team.*

6 DEIREADH FÓMHAIR / 6 OCTOBER

Dúshlán
Challenge

[doo-hlawn]

An bhfuil tú inniúil don dúshlán?
Are you up to the challenge?

Dúshlán is the word you need for a physical or mental challenge, a marathon to be run or a boardroom to be conquered. I never use it when I'm talking about sports. There's no better preparation for a GAA team in pre-season than the good aul 'challenge match', but please don't say *dúshlán* in that context. The physical challenge has to be more extreme. We are getting down to the nitty-gritty of the specific times this Irish word can be used.

Dúshlán is the type of challenge when you're all sitting in a meeting room talking about a big project, and someone says, 'Right, we're getting nowhere, lads. We have to go back to square one.' You have to clean up the mess, redo everything. Walking up Croagh Patrick is a challenge, but if you're one of those people who decide to do it barefoot, it's a double *dúshlán*. It's a mountain to be climbed, both physically and mentally.

7 DEIREADH FÓMHAIR / 7 OCTOBER

Ag teacht agus ag imeacht
Coming and going

[egg chawkht ah-gus egg im-okht]

Bhí slua seasta ag teacht agus ag imeacht an t-am ar fad ag an tsochraid mhór áitiúil.
There was a steady crowd coming and going all the time at the big local funeral.

Irish people are always either coming or going. If you're not coming home from somewhere, you're heading off somewhere. The mind and the legs are always working. It's like we've solved perpetual motion. 'God, I have to go to the shops and then bring the eldest lad to training and then the youngest girl has a match after that. Then we have to be at the sister's house for dinner, but I need to swing by the brother-in-law's to collect the chainsaw on the way.' If your body isn't coming and going, you're thinking about all the coming and going it has to do later.

And when everything mounts up, you might even say, 'I don't know whether I'm coming or going.' They're the hallowed words of an Irish mother. How do you explain that phrase to someone from far-flung lands learning English? To be *ag teacht agus ag imeacht* is embedded in our culture. We don't know how to sit still. Now I'm off to get the dinner on, because I've to go to the club to coach the Junior Bs later ...

8 DEIREADH FÓMHAIR / 8 OCTOBER

Éad
Jealousy

[aid]

Tá éad orm go bhfuil tú ag imeacht ar do laethanta saoire go ceann míosa.
I'm so jealous that you're off on a month's holidays.

This is a powerful three-letter word that means exactly what it says on the tin. It sounds like a brand-new TG4 drama set in deepest Connemara, where murder and jealousy reign supreme as a wealthy fishing family's multimillion-euro trawler is set on fire one night ... 'Éad, anocht ag leathuair tar éis a naoi ar TG4.'

9 DEIREADH FÓMHAIR / 9 OCTOBER

Ag feitheamh/ag fanacht
Waiting

[eg feh-hiv/egg fan-okht]

Bhí mé ag feitheamh taobh amuigh de chlinic an fhiaclóra.
I was waiting outside the dentist's clinic.

It's totally up to you which one to use. They basically mean the same thing, with a slight difference. You might remember *fanacht* if you did Irish in school, but *feitheamh* might be new to you. *Feitheamh* is the type of waiting that takes place on a platform, when your boyfriend is about to arrive on the five o'clock train from Galway. It's waiting at the door of the restaurant for the rest of the gang to arrive before you go inside. There's a feeling of anticipation about *feitheamh*; it's in the moment, waiting for the bus to come because you're already running late. Or better yet, you're *ag feitheamh* outside the test centre for your driving test to start. Now that's *real* anticipation.

Ag fanacht is waiting around for the plumber to come, when they say they'll be with you 'sometime after lunch' and you know in reality that's a window of about five hours. You can get on with other things, as long as you stay at home.

In English, all you can do is wait, but in Irish, you can be *ag feitheamh* or you can be *ag fanacht,* depending on how you feel at the time.

10 DEIREADH FÓMHAIR / 10 OCTOBER

Foirfe
Perfect

[fwir-if-a]

An eol duit cá bhfuil an teach, uimhir 46? Is eol? Foirfe.
Do you know where the house is, number 46? You do? Perfect.

This is one you can definitely throw into your daily conversations. *Foirfe* is the 'sound', 'got ya', 'copy that' moment. You can say it when someone gives you all the details you need: 'We're meeting in Covent Garden at 7 p.m. on 10 October.' '*Foirfe*. See ya then.'

Try to end your phone calls with it, end your texts with it, use it when you bump into your neighbour on the street. Your friends might say, 'What's that?', but once you tell them, they'll know it too and they might pass it on. This is how a language recovers and gathers momentum, by being used in your friend and work circles. You don't have to be having full conversations *as Gaeilge*. Slip Irish words into your English conversations as much as you can, and eventually they will become the norm. We're long past *Conas atá tú?* at this stage; let's jump on the wave of *foirfe*.

11 DEIREADH FÓMHAIR / 11 OCTOBER

Dorn
Fist

[durr-un]

Rinne sé dorn lena lámh.
He made a fist with his hand.

12 DEIREADH FÓMHAIR / 12 OCTOBER

Beir greim air
Catch it, grab hold of it

[ber grime err]

Beir greim air sin dom, le do thoil.
Hold that there for me, please.

In any Gaeltacht summer course in any part of the country, when all the *coláiste* is out playing sports on those long, sunny afternoons, you will hear *Beir greim air*! being shouted by the *cinnirí* and the *cúntóirí*. It's a staple, meat-and-two-veg phrase, but there's so much movement in it. It can be used when you catch someone as they run past you in game of tag, or when you ask someone to hold something for you, like a tradesman to his junior apprentice: 'Hold that hammer for me there for a sec.'

Beir greim air is a vice grip. You know you need to take care of whatever you're holding if this phrase is used. Like someone asking you to hold their baby or their pint – and what's more important in life than babies and pints? You'll never let them fall.

13 DEIREADH FÓMHAIR / 13 OCTOBER

Leadóg bhoird
Table tennis

[lad-owg vord]

Thaitin leadóg bhoird go mór liom nuair a bhí me ar scoil.
I loved table tennis when I was at school.

I was a disciple of ping-pong when I was in primary school. There would be two or three table-tennis tables going full ping-pong every lunchtime in the hall. I even had a special holder for my bat. The height of my table-tennis career was when I beat Alan Reilly to become the table-tennis champion of my school. I was especially proud because he was in sixth class and I was only in fourth class. I had perfected the Chinese serve, which is when you kind of shield the ball behind your hand before you fling it really high in the air. It completely bamboozles your opponent. There weren't many people doing the Chinese serve in Navan, so it was the key to my victory.

I then got the chance to test my skills in a ping-pong club in Singapore when we went there to film the travel show. There were about 30 or 40 children in Glyx Sports Table Tennis Academy, all training to be champions. The sound of ping-pong was everywhere; I was in my element. The coach was training a little six-year-old girl and I've never seen anything like it. You could just about see her ponytail bouncing above the table, but she was phenomenal, so we decided I should hold a couple of rallies with her. I tried my trademark Chinese serve on her and she just laughed at me. I hadn't a chance. But I'm still proud of beating Alan Reilly when I was in fourth class. He's a pharmacist now, but I never let him get by me without reminding him that I beat him comprehensively at *leadóg bhoird*.

14 DEIREADH FÓMHAIR / 14 OCTOBER

Eochair
Key

[ukk-er]

Chaill me eochair an tí an tseachtain seo caite.
I lost the key of the house last week.

Me, my mam and my brother Mark were going to a cousin's wedding, so I booked us a minibus to take us from the bungalow in Navan to the venue. I was the last out of the house in my three-piece suit and I made sure to lock the door.

We have a great time at the wedding, and the minibus drops us back home at three in the morning. It pulls away and I go to my pocket for the house key, but it's not there and we can't find a spare. Outside your front door at three in the morning with no key isn't where you want to be with your mother when she's been on her feet in high heels all day, and it just got worse and worse and worse. I ring the minibus to ask it to come back, and I scour the floor on my hands and knees. Nothing. At this stage we've been outside the front door for over an hour, so I say to my mother, 'We'll have to get a hotel.' A hotel in our own town? Her face was like soured milk.

I get a taxi to the locksmiths early the next morning and we drive out to the house in his van, and when he checks the lock, he tells me he can't open it; it's too old. He has to break the window in the back door. Jesus Christ almighty! I drive to the hotel to break the news to my mother and bring her home to an open door and a smashed window.

I've been in my suit for over 24 hours at this stage, so I go to have a shower, and when I take my jacket off, I notice something: on the inside of the jacket is one of those slitty little pockets, and inside it is the *eochair* to the front door. It had been on me the whole time. I never told my mother.

15 DEIREADH FÓMHAIR / 15 OCTOBER

Céasta
Excruciating

[kay-sta]

Bhuail mé mo bharraicín ar bhun na leapa. Bhí me céasta leis an bpian.
I hit my toe off the bottom of the bed. The pain was excruciating.

I was travelling through Malaysia, heading for the island of Penang. The capital is Georgetown, an old, colonial-style harbour town that looks like it's seen better days. You could say the same for the hotels; they probably would have been great in the 1970s and '80s when they were decorated, but now were just barely getting by. The hotel we stayed in was fusty, something like an old Chinese boarding house, and the rooms were full of huge wooden furniture from decades ago. But as long as the sheets were clean and the shower was good, I was grand.

The bed was a large four-poster yoke, high off the ground on chunky legs. In the middle of the night, in the pitch black, I had to go to the toilet. My bearings weren't a hundred per cent, so I was feeling my way around. You know when you go to the toilet in the middle of the night and when you're done you want to quickly hop back into bed? Well, I returned to the bed at speed and stubbed my little toe full force on the chunky leg post. It was as if a bolt of lightning shot up my toe. An excruciating, throbbing pain that wouldn't go away.

The next morning, when I got to examine the damage, there was blood everywhere, my toe was black and purple, and the nail was gone. It looked like it had come out of a zombie apocalypse. Now that's what *céasta* is – not any aul pain, but to be crucified with pain.

16 DEIREADH FÓMHAIR / 16 OCTOBER

Trátaí
Tomatoes

[traw-tee]

Ní féidir sailéad ceart a ithe gan trátaí.
You can't have a decent salad without tomatoes.

We buy our fair share of tomatoes in this house. We have a big bowl of them on the windowsill all the time. They're great for a cold-meat salad, and if you grew up in Ireland, you were brought up on cold-meat salads.

Every time my in-laws come over for a Sunday roast, we make a big roast beef with all the trimmings. The plates are overflowing with carrots, parsnips, potatoes, croquettes and gravy, and we'll always have a pavlova or apple tart with fresh cream for afters. But they still can't go home to Clare without having a cold-meat salad. We have to make sure they're fed for their journey home, even though it's only 45 minutes down the road. So two hours after the roast, we start all over again with the sliced ham, coleslaw, leftover potatoes, scallions and loads and loads of big, fat *trátaí*.

17 DEIREADH FÓMHAIR / 17 OCTOBER

Pionta
A *pint*

[pyun-ta]

Is breá liom pionta pórtair i mo phub áitiúil.
I love a pint of porter in my local pub.

If you're in Connemara, you pronounce this 'pin-ta', but if you're in Dingle speaking Munster Irish, it's pronounced 'pyun-ta'. But they're both talking about the same thing – a lovely pint.

I had no interest in Guinness in my 20s or 30s. It was only when Tommy said to me, many years ago now, when he was just back on the drink, 'Will we go for a pint?' and we met in The Crane Bar in Galway. We ordered two pints of Guinness and I swear to God, I think that night I entered Narnia. By my second pint, I had the keys to the kingdom. It was as if Irishness was filling me up with every sip.

Years later, when me, Tommy and Laurita were doing our *Three Pints Please* podcast, we would go into the little pub for that week at ten in the morning and there would be silence. We were supposed to be recording a podcast, but no one was talking – all you could hear was the hiss of the taps as they poured our Guinness. The pints would come down, we would take a drink, and then we would make the podcast. Guinness brings a level of cosiness and giddiness, and that's when stories start spilling out of people's mouths. When you're on your second pint on a Monday morning and it's not even midday, and there's a little fire going in the corner and I'm sitting with Tommy and Laurita, it feels like there's no one else in the world. I really do appreciate a *pionta* of stout now.

18 DEIREADH FÓMHAIR / 18 OCTOBER

Teach tábhairne
Pub

[chok tao-or-nya]

Tá seanteach tábhairne a bhí dúnta ar oscailt arís.
An old pub that was closed is open again.

When you're speaking Irish, it's totally acceptable to just say 'pub', but I want to give you the real name for 'pub' in Irish. *Teach tábhairne* translates more as 'tavern house', which sounds cosier and more welcoming than 'pub'. A place where ale is drunk and songs are sung.

In Jamaica, all the pubs are called taverns. We were there filming the travel show and I was walking along Treasure Beach, an idyllic little resort, looking at a fisherman fixing his net, when I noticed a little tavern right on the beach. We walked in and had a cold beer, and I saw a sign hanging on the wall that said 'Tavern Regulations'. I got talking to the woman behind the bar and I asked her if she lived here, and she said, 'No, no. I live next door. But people do live here if they get drunk.' 'What?' I said. I couldn't believe it. She explained that according to the tavern laws in Jamaica, if someone is drunk on your premises, you have to have a special room for them so they can sleep it off in the bar.

'You're fucking kidding me,' I said.

'No,' she said. 'I have two rooms for people who get drunk and it's been that way since the eighteenth century.'

Can you imagine that in your local pub in Ireland? They might not have anything like that in a pub, but I can see it in a *teach tábhairne*.

19 DEIREADH FÓMHAIR / 19 OCTOBER

Deoch an dorais
One for the road

[jyukh on dur-ish]

Bhí seisiún maith ann aréir; bhí deoch an dorais againn timpeall a haon ar maidin.
There was a great session on last night; we had one for the road around one in the morning.

This literally means 'a drink at the door'. It's the last one when you know the craic is good, when you're enjoying the company, the spontaneous night has developed and you look to your partner or your friend and say, 'Will we have one for the road?' Very few people say no to *deoch an dorais*.

20 DEIREADH FÓMHAIR / 20 OCTOBER

Im
Butter

[im]

Níl rud ar bith níos fearr ná im ar arán donn baile.
There's nothing better than butter on homemade brown bread.

21 DEIREADH FÓMHAIR / 21 OCTOBER

Aigne, intinn
Mind

[ag-na, in-tinn]

Bhí sé i m'aigne rud éicint a rá ag an gcruinniú.
It was in my mind to say something at the meeting.
Bhí sé ar a hintinn aici.
It was on her mind.

Where is the mind? How deep is it in our heads? Your *ceann* is your head, and *aigne* is the word for what's deep inside it. Our *aigne* is where our thoughts and feelings are, where we make sense of stuff. I think of our mind like a warm room inside our heads, and it's full of stories and jokes and compassion. If the brain is the factory, the mind is the break room with the lovely coffee and soft furnishings – it's always there, but you can only access it sometimes. I'm happiest when my mind is happy. We should all let our mind wander, so it will hopefully land on things that make us content.

Intinn is another word for 'mind' in Irish. The differences are subtle, barely there. *Aigne* and *intinn* are fairly interchangeable, the creative part and the function part of our thinking, side by side.

22 DEIREADH FÓMHAIR / 22 OCTOBER

Teannas
Tension

[chan-ass]

Bhí teannas dochreidte sa scannán.
There was some unreal tension in the film.

When something is *teann* in Irish, it's stretched to the limit, so *teannas* is like that elastic band that's almost at snapping point. When you walk into a meeting and something's about to kick off, or when you're watching a film and nobody is speaking, everyone is glued to the screen, then you know there's *teannas*.

23 DEIREADH FÓMHAIR / 23 OCTOBER

Copóg shráide
Dock leaf

[cup-owg hraw-ja]

D'úsaid mé copóg shráide théis mo lámh a chur sna neantóga.
I used a dock leaf after putting my hand into the nettles.

For me, the dock leaf is one of the great living leaf-weeds of our lands. It flourishes during the summer months. Where you see nettles, you see dock leaves. It's the Savlon of the natural world. Every child brought up in Ireland should know the power of the **copóg** shráide.

24 DEIREADH FÓMHAIR / 24 OCTOBER

Neantóg
Nettle

[nyan-towg]

Tá cumhacht iontach sa neantóg.
There is great power in the nettle.

Nettles were your arch-enemy when you were a child. You were always worried about them: either getting stung or trying not to get stung. A few years ago when I was out in the garden, I got stung by nettles, and it was like I'd jumped in a time machine that brought me back to the age of eight or nine and what it felt like to be stung then. And it was exhilarating, because I wasn't afraid of being stung by nettles any more. I enjoyed seeing the little white dots come up on my skin. The nettles that stung me looked really healthy, and they must have been three feet tall, so I decided to cut them and bring them into the podcast studio the next day to sting Tommy and Laurita.

So I smuggled them into the Hen House in a plastic bag, and when we started recording, I produced the nettles. Tommy and Laurita looked at me and were like, 'What the hell is this?' 'I'm going to sting you with these nettles,' I said. 'When's the last time you were stung by a nettle?' They thought I was mad, but they said okay, and the fear they had of being stung by nettles was still there. So I brushed their hands with the nettles and their skin just erupted, and they were brought back in a time machine to when they were kids, when *neantóga* were in abundance in fields and cracks in footpaths. It was extreme podcasting, like *Dirty Sanchez* Irish country-style, but it sparked a great conversation. And I had the *copóga sráide* (dock leaves, p. 284) at the ready to heal the stings.

25 DEIREADH FÓMHAIR / 25 OCTOBER

Tiompán na cluaise
Eardrum

[tyump-awn na cloo-sha]

Bhí pian dhamanta i dtiompán mo chluaise.
I had an awful pain in my eardrum.

You can hear the 'thump' in tiompán na cluaise. *Everything in this phrase has to do with the sound that comes through your ear. You can practically hear the reverberations when you say it.*

26 DEIREADH FÓMHAIR / 26 OCTOBER

Sciobtha
Nifty

[*shkyup-ee*]

Bhí an cailín óg sciobtha leis an liathróid.
The young girl was nifty with the football.

This could be one of the best-sounding words in the book, if you ask me. It's a hundred per cent West of Ireland and as pure a *Gaeilge Chonamara* word as any. The minute it leaves the mouth, it sounds rapid. It's an event that happens in the blink of an eye – a fast greyhound breaking from the traps, a nippy corner forward, a teacher telling the kids to hurry along back to class.

Even in English, 'nifty' and 'nippy' are different kinds of fast. It speaks to agility and movement, like driving a Peugeot 205 GTI down a windy country road in 1986. And we all know someone in school who was *sciobtha*; no one could touch them for speed.

27 DEIREADH FÓMHAIR / 27 OCTOBER

Ceangal
A connection

[kyan-gul]

Tá ceangal againn ar fad leis an talamh agus an bhfharraige.
We all have a connection with the land and the sea.

Ceangal *is the link we all need – to family, friends, our work, the land. It's a bond. This is a great word for any Leaving Cert students who want to impress. Slip it into the Irish orals and you're guaranteed a few extra marks; trust me.*

28 DEIREADH FÓMHAIR / 28 OCTOBER

Giolcach
Reed

[gyul-kokh]

Bíonn an ghiolcach ag fás sa tSionainn.
The reed grows in the Shannon.

Reed, the Inquisitor
28 OCTOBER–24 NOVEMBER

If you were born between now and 24 November, your Celtic tree is the reed. Reed people like to get to the bottom of things. They sit down with a cup of tea and hear the full story. If you want to get to know your Celtic birth tree, head to a river or a lake and spend some time alone with the tall reeds poking their feathery heads above water. Even better, reeds were used to make thatched roofs, so find yourself a nice cottage for a long weekend and your Celtic birth sign will be right over your head.

29 DEIREADH FÓMHAIR / 29 OCTOBER

Athair thalún
Yarrow

[a-hur hall-oon]

Fásann an athair thalún go flúirseach amuigh faoin tuath.
Yarrow grows in abundance in the countryside.

30 DEIREADH FÓMHAIR / 30 OCTOBER

Ag filleadh abhaile
Returning home

[egg fill-a a-wal-ya]

Bhí an cailín ag filleadh abhaile tar éis cúig bliana san Astráil.
The girl was returning home after five years in Australia.

This isn't coming home from town after a night out or from Tesco after doing the big shop. It has all the heavyweight feeling of returning home after a long time, the ones coming back after having left the country to seek their fortunes elsewhere. This is embracing your son or daughter at Dublin or Shannon Airport after a long absence.

31 DEIREADH FÓMHAIR / 31 OCTOBER

Cailleach
Witch

[kyle-yokh]

Bhí sean-chailleach ina cónaí san fhoraois fadó.
An old witch lived in the forest long ago.

To me, a witch isn't the woman with the pointy hat on the broomstick, it's the person who understands the land and Mother Nature. Everyone needs the old-school witch with the cauldron for Halloween, but some modern cailleacha *have swapped the cauldron for a pestle and mortar. They're known as* cailleacha an chlaí, *'hedge witches', and they know all about herbal medicine.*

1 SAMHAIN / 1 NOVEMBER

Cur isteach ar
To disturb/bother

[kur ish-tokh air]

Tá brón orm cur isteach ort, ach ...
Sorry to bother you, but ...

Cur isteach ort almost translates as 'put in on you'. That's the power of description in the Irish language; if someone is *ag cur isteach ort*, you know straight away that it's an imposition. I doubt our tribal ancestors ever used this phrase, because you wouldn't have clans walking up to each other saying, 'Sorry to disturb you ...' And when the Vikings came to plunder Ireland's resources, they had no bother disturbing us. They'd just chop your head off. This is a modern phrase, born out of corporate PAs to big honcho CEOs. PAs have to disturb their bosses all the time, so if you want to do it politely in Irish, keep *cur isteach ort* in your back pocket.

I hear 'Sorry to bother you' the odd time when I'm in SuperValu trying to decide which kind of Donegal Catch to buy. I'll be picking up and putting down the haddock and the whiting and the breaded cod, and I'll hear, 'Hector, sorry to disturb you, but I absolutely adored the story about the mobile classroom in the Philippines. I really enjoy the shows. Thank you, bye.' But I really hope people will *cuir isteach orm*. It's the loveliest thing in the world when someone disturbs you from your stupid head and your daily routine to say something nice to you. I want to be able to disturb someone to give them a compliment, and I think we should all have the openness and humility to engage with each other for those few seconds. If we don't swap these little moments, where will we end up? I get my energy from *cur isteach ort* conversations.

2 SAMHAIN / 2 NOVEMBER

Anam
Soul

[on-um]

Chuir sé a chroí agus a anam isteach sa jab.
He put his heart and soul into the job.

The 'n' and 'm' in anam *give it so much depth: 'on-um'. It sounds like the Irish entry to the Eurovision Song Contest. It's a word that comes from deep within. We think of James Brown as having soul, but we all have soul – it's that brilliant, beautiful, intangible thing that's inside us.*

3 SAMHAIN / 3 NOVEMBER

Maidneachan
Dawn

[my-na-khun]

Théis na stoirme aréir, bhris an ghrian amach ag an maidneachan.
After the storm last night, the sun broke at dawn.

A word from deepest Connemara – the likes of Leitir Mealláin and Leitir Móir – that describes that gap between night and day, the reset of Mother Nature as the sun is yet to rise. No one is up apart from the working people of Connemara, down at the beach beside their boats, when colour is coming back into the sky and they're about to head out. That moment of light is completely different in Connemara to other parts of the world, so why wouldn't they have their own way of describing it?

4 SAMHAIN / 4 NOVEMBER

Triomadóir rothlaim
Tumble dryer

[trum-a-dor ruh-hlum]

An bhfuil rud níos fearr ann ná triomadóir rothlaim lán d'éadaí tirime?
Is there a better thing than a tumble dryer full of dry clothes?

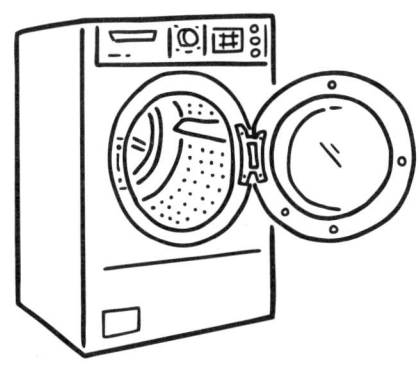

5 SAMHAIN / 5 NOVEMBER

Mhúscail sé
He awoke

[voos-kil shay]

Mhúscail an leabhar seo an Ghaeilge a bhí ionam.
This book awoke the Irish that was inside me.

Mhúscail sé has nothing to do with sleep. It's more about waking the gods, the land or the heavens. It's a phrase for myths and legends, the ancients lying deep within the Hill of Tara suddenly opening their eyes. It's difficult to explain, but I suppose it's otherworldly. It's like the sun rising for the first time after a nuclear holocaust, or a six-year-old who has had the mother of all sleeps after being up all night with a tummy bug: 'He awoke!' If Gandalf from *The Lord of the Rings* were a *Gaeilgeoir*, he would use this.

You can also use it to describe a passion that has stirred inside of you. Something that had been lying dormant, until one day you got up and started painting or writing or creating something. *Mhúscail sé* is an epic phrase for an epic event.

6 SAMHAIN / 6 NOVEMBER

Brúitín
Mashed potato

[bru-teen]

Brúitín, mairteoil rósta, píseanna agus cairéid le súlach.
Mashed potato, roast beef, peas and carrots with gravy.

How good are we at making mashed potato? The level of culinary skill we have when it comes to making mash is unreal. How many tonnes do we make a week, from Wexford to Tralee, Dublin to Sligo, Cork to Donegal? Ireland has to be the mashed potato HQ of the world. Happiness is when you come in on a Sunday for your roast and see a mound of mash on the plate, or when you go to your favourite pub for the carvery and they're generous with their scoops. The delight on a child's face when Mammy or Daddy has made the mashed potato just right is pure joy.

There's a creativity in what chefs and mammies add to their mash, the level of milk and butter, the salt and pepper, the secret ingredients ... I like to add a little bit of Colman's mustard to my mash. It gives it a nice zing. I've increased the level of flavour in my mash over the years to get my boys' palates used to it, and now that they're 19 and 21, they can handle the dollop of Colman's. Every time I do it, the youngest lad will look at me and go, 'You were at the mustard again, were you?' Everyone loves their own homemade version of mashed potato. I tell you one thing, you could nearly have a *brúitín* documentary because of the depth of our love for the stuff.

7 **SAMHAIN** / 7 NOVEMBER

Bogach
Marsh

[bug-okh]

Tá an talamh sa ghleann ina bogach.
The land in the valley is marsh.

———————————

This is a word you need wellies for. It reminds me of the word for muck, puiteach, *which I had in* The Irish Words You Should Know. *They both sound squishy and squashy, like you're walking in the Twelve Bens or the Comeragh Mountains or up Errigal, and to get to the next part of the trail you have to cross a marsh. Bog means 'soft', so there's a softness to* bogach, *a squelch. It sounds like what it means.*

8 SAMHAIN / 8 NOVEMBER

Dúchasach
Native

[doo-ka-sockh]

Tá na Navachóigh i measc mhuintir dhúchasach Mheiriceá Thuaidh.
The Navajo are natives of North America.

I spent time on a Navajo reservation in Arizona for the TG4 travel show. The Navajo were one of the most powerful Indigenous tribes and their land stretched on for thousands of miles, all through Arizona and Colorado. The reservation now is sparse and sad, but I met a very special lady there. She was a granny in her 70s who drove a 15,000-gallon water tanker all around the reservation twice a week. I was waiting for her on the road outside the reservation, and along she came in her massive tanker and beeped the horn. I jumped in and spent the next six hours with her delivering water to remote parts of the reservation. The people there have no services and no amenities – it's like stepping back in time about 300 years – but this lady made sure everyone could fill their tanks with fresh and clean water. She even had lollipops for the kids.

I suppose I have mixed feelings about the word 'native'; I don't think I really like it. It sounds like someone came up with it while looking at people through binoculars. But *dúchasach* brings more of a richness to it, because it's formed from *dúchas*, which means 'heritage'. It's a lot nicer a word than 'native', that's for sure.

9 SAMHAIN / 9 NOVEMBER

Fonn
Inclination, mood; tune, melody

[fown]

An bhfuil fonn ort dul amach anocht?
Are you in the mood to go out tonight?

Fonn has a double meaning, and when you get into the nitty-gritty of it, you can see how the meanings are connected. It can be used to say you're in the mood for something, but also to describe getting used to playing a tune. If someone asks you, '*Cad é an fonn sin?*' (What's that tune?), they don't want the name of the song, they want to know how it goes. It's a phrase perfect for the beauty of Irish trad music, where a musician only has to listen to a tune a couple of times before they pick it up. There's no sheet music here; it's about playing by ear.

So when it comes to your mood, *An bhfuil fonn ort?* is like asking, 'Is your body in tune?' Are your body and mind vibrating at the same frequency? Are your endorphins flowing? Is your energy in rhythm?'

Being in the *fonn* for something opens up possibility, but you have to listen to your inner melody to know whether you're in the form of doing something or not. *Fonn* is the lilting of an Irish tune and the lilting of your mood. What a beautiful word.

10 SAMHAIN / 10 NOVEMBER

Roithleagán ró
Merry-go-round

[roh-hla-gawn roe]

Bhí na páistí ag súgradh ar an roithleagán ró.
The children were playing on the merry-go-round.

11 SAMHAIN / 11 NOVEMBER

Tinneas cinn
Headache

[tinn-iss keen]

Bhí tinneas cinn damanta orm inné tar éis na hoibre.
I had an awful headache yesterday after work.

This is the headache you get from a lack of sleep or a lack of water or a three-hour Zoom call. It's not alcohol-related – that's cloigeann tinn, *featured in* The Irish Words You Should Know. Tinneas cinn *is purely medical, the 'Where's the ibuprofen?' kind of headache.*

12 SAMHAIN / 12 NOVEMBER

Síothlán caife
Coffee percolator

[shee-uh-lawn kafay]

Bhris an síothlán caife ag an obair.
The coffee percolator at work broke.

I can't drink coffee at home; I can only drink it if I'm out. I'm a tea man at home and a coffee man on the roam. I won't even drink it if I'm in someone else's house. My granny taught me to drink tea at the age of eight, and I haven't stopped. I like to think of my house as a spiritual tea house. There's nothing nicer when your friends call around and you get chatting and go through pots of the stuff.

Having said that, I love finding little coffee shops in the middle of nowhere. When I'm on the road for three months of the year filming the travel show, I'll drink coffee all the time. When we're way up north in Broome in Australia and there's nothing around for miles, I'm the one Googling for a coffee shop. We have become coffee lunatics in Ireland. A lot of GAA clubs have their own barista at this stage, so you can stand on the sidelines sipping a flat white while the sacred game is played. Nescafé granules used to be good enough for us, but if you walk into a café now and say, 'Can I have a coffee?' they'll look at you like you have two heads. You have to know your coffee lingo. Even the classic *síothlán caife* has been relegated to factory canteens and teachers' lounges.

13 SAMHAIN / 13 NOVEMBER

Marla
Plasticine

[mawr-la]

Is cuimhin liom marla nuair a bhí mé ar an mbunscoil.
I remember marla when I was in primary school.

The teachers of the 1970s and '80s didn't have many resources, but they always had *marla*. All the kids in their classes became little Michelangelos. The smell of the stuff will bring you right back to a creative time in your childhood, when you first pulled those blue and red and green and orange strips off the packet and rolled them between your hands to make something completely new. You'd be sitting at the table with your best little buddies sculpting tiny people and flowers and animals out of plasticine. I bet you didn't even hear the word 'plasticine' when you were a child; it was always just *marla* – the Irish word was *the* word.

Then Play-Doh came on the scene and things started to get technical. It came with cutters and scalpels and machinery. Someone should have got hold of the brand name Marla and driven it to be one of the greatest modelling clay companies in the world, but Play-Doh made it too hard. So here's to the national school teachers who took out the *marla* on a Friday afternoon in school. I hope those colourful strips of possibility can still be found in the fists of junior infants all around the country.

14 SAMHAIN / 14 NOVEMBER

Spleodrach
Feisty, exuberant

[splow-drokh]

Bhí cluiche spleodrach idir an dá fhoireann.
There was a feisty game between the two teams.

This word is like inner dynamite. It makes me think of a boiling pot of spuds where the water is bubbling over the side, so you need to run to it immediately to take it off the heat – spleodrach *is that in human form; they're ready to blow at any time. There's a feeling of energy to it.*

15 SAMHAIN / 15 NOVEMBER

Slisíní bagúin
Rashers

[slish-ee-nee baw-goo-in]

Is maith liom ceapaire le slisíní bagúin.
I love a rasher sandwich.

We only ever have rashers on a Saturday morning in my house. It all started when the lads got their football boots for GAA and soccer at around four or five years of age. They would have matches on Saturdays and Sundays, religiously, always early mornings and always freezing cold. Then when you got the boys home, by the time they were out of the dirty shorts and shin pads and football boots, I'd have the bath running. They'd be sitting in the bath warming up and they'd know that the fry was on downstairs. The grill would be heavy with sausages, rashers, and black and white pudding, the smell wafting through the house, because Saturday morning was fry time.

There's no way any Irish person can say no to a rasher and sausage, a bit of pudding, brown sauce, a slice of toast and a cup of tea on a Saturday morning. That, to me, is the heavenly food of the weekend. Now that we have an air fryer, there's BLTs flying all over the place to make the most of the lovely *slisíní bagúin*.

And here's a bonus word for you: *slisín* means 'slice', so you can use it for a slice of bread (*slisín arán*) or a slice of cake (*slisín cáca*).

16 SAMHAIN / 16 NOVEMBER

Cíos
Rent

[kee-uss]

D'ardaigh an tiarna talún an cíos ar an árasán.
The landlord raised the rent on the flat.

'Rent' is a word that doesn't exactly bring up nice feelings. We've all paid rent at some point; it's part and parcel of life. *Cíos* has been around since the beginning of time, but the word has become more powerful as the years have gone on. But I want to talk about the other things we rent, the things that bring joy into our lives, like renting a bicycle on the Aran Islands, a moped in Thailand or a gondola in Venice.

The idea of renting something will always bring me back to the days of Xtra-vision and the front-loading VHS player in our house in Navan. In a small country town, Xtra-vision was like a cultural hive. It brought the world to you. You'd go down to the local Xtra-vision with your laminated membership card and the walls would be covered in racks and racks of tapes, but we'd head straight for the new releases. Me and my brothers agreed on what to rent as well; as long as there was blood and guts and violence in it, it was for us. There was always a heavy metal dude or punk girl behind the counter who'd dole out the fines if you were late returning your tape. Renting a movie was a big part of the weekend back then, and going to your local Xtra-vision was as important as going to your local chipper. It was a Friday night pilgrimage.

17 SAMHAIN / 17 NOVEMBER

Cipín
Match

[kip-een]

Las an seanfhear an cipín ag an doras.
The old man lit the match at the door.

You can use this word to describe kindling, the small little sticks that you start a fire with, but mostly it's used for the good aul Irish match. A group of men in suits and caps leaning against a wall outside of mass, lighting their pipes with their *cipíní*. A *cipín* was known back then as a smoking match, and we had a box of them on the mantlepiece of homes all over the country. They made the flames that lit the fires that warmed generations.

We have been making matches in Ireland for over a hundred years. They had Bo Peep matches up North, but we always had the iconic yellow box of Cara matches from Maguire & Paterson. There was a small box you could keep in your pocket and the big box of long safety matches that were handy for the old-style gas cooker in the kitchen. I never liked the smell of a match, that moment when oxygen and sulphur collide, but before firelighters and Zippos, the Cara *cipín* lit up the nation.

18 SAMHAIN / 18 NOVEMBER

Ráca
Rake

[raw-ka]

Sheas mé ar an ráca inné.
I stood on the rake yesterday.

19 SAMHAIN / 19 NOVEMBER

Timpeallán
Roundabout

[teem-pa-lawn]

Tá an iomarca timpeallán againn in Éirinn.
We have too many roundabouts in Ireland.

Let's talk about the 177,564 roundabouts we have in Ireland. They are the greatest creation of every county councillor. We must salute the men and women on county councils in the 1950s and '60s who were sitting there looking at town plans and said, 'I know what we need: more roundabouts.' Galway is a Mecca for roundabouts. The City of the Tribes has a roundabout for every tribe, but none of them can hold a candle to the famous roundabouts of Ireland. AA Roadwatch has made the likes of the Walkinstown Roundabout and the Dunkettle Roundabout national landmarks. They're like the Cliffs of Moher for commuters. The evolution of the Red Cow Roundabout alone was a feat of engineering. It was a simple roundabout 40 years ago and now it can be seen from space.

Then someone invented the mini-roundabout, just so we can fit more in. We are fixated with them. I know there's someone on a county council somewhere who still thinks roundabouts are the future, so let's start a campaign to make Ireland *timpeallán*-free by 2060.

20 SAMHAIN / 20 NOVEMBER

Ag crith
Shaking

[egg krih]

Bhí an madra ag crith leis an bhfuacht taobh amuigh den doras.
The dog was shaking with the cold outside the door.

As our Jack Russell, Rocco, gets older, when we send him outside for his wee, he'll look at us as if to say, 'Are you for real?' He'll go out, have his wee, and come straight around to the window so he can put on this little body shake to guilt us into letting him back in. And eventually we'll break. The crith *always gets us.*

21 SAMHAIN / 21 NOVEMBER

Bualadh leathair
Sexual intercourse

[boo-la lah-her]

Bhí go leor bualadh leathair sa scannán aréir.
There was a load of sex in the movie last night.

This literally means 'hitting leather', and you can say bualadh craicinn (*hitting skin*) *too. If TG4 added some raunchy movies late on a Friday night, you could say there was* bualadh leathar ar TG4 (*boo-la lah-her air tee jee ca-her*)!

22 SAMHAIN / 22 NOVEMBER

Mairteoil
Beef

[mar-chole]

Bhí píosa álainn mairteola againn ar an Domhnach.
We had a lovely bit of beef on Sunday.

It takes a lot of saucepans to make a roast dinner, so we should celebrate them. The oven is on all day with the beef and the roasties, and all the trimmings need to be prepared and cooked. Sundays always meant mass and roast dinners; now we don't have the mass as much, but we still have the roasts. If you've been out all day working or training, there's nothing nicer than coming home in the evening and your roast is in the oven waiting for you. The saucepans have been cleaned, the dishwasher has been emptied, but the dinner has been kept for you.

Roasts are the pillar of Irish households, and the carving of the beef is ritualistic. My dad would come in every Sunday to carve the roast, and we were fancy, so we had an electric carving knife. It was one of those great appliances that infiltrated millions of homes around the UK and Ireland in the 1980s. It was always a dad's job to carve the roast, and I do the carving now in my house. There's something about a roast *mairteoil* dinner that's sacred in Ireland. It sparks emotion.

23 SAMHAIN / 23 NOVEMBER

Poitigéir
Chemist

[put-ih-gair]

Tá aithne mhaith agam ar an bpoitigéir áitiúil sa bhaile.
I know the local chemist in the town well.

Everyone knows their local chemist; you have a relationship with them. They know your prescriptions and they know the names of your children and where you went on holiday. We always went to a chemist in Navan called McConnell's, which had a lovely old-school black wooden shopfront. It gave the feeling that there were tinctures and potions inside, instead of boxes of paracetamol.

When we're away filming, I'm the chemist of the group. I have Fucibet cream for the bites, Dioralyte, Imodium … If anyone has a problem, I'll probably have the antidote in my bag. When we were filming in Australia, we went to a chemist to stock up and it was like a warehouse. There's a chain actually called Chemist Warehouse and it's like IKEA for medicine; it must have been about 50,000 square foot. You can get a bit addicted to them, because they have so much good stuff to buy; there were products that I didn't even know existed. We'd love dossing in there for a few minutes looking at the thousand different vitamins and nail clippers and bandages. But I wouldn't want to be going there if I have a problem that needs a conversation.

What you really want from your chemist is to be able to go in and say, 'How are ya, Margaret. I've a terrible itchy arsehole,' and for them to answer, 'No worries, Bridie. I'll get the Preparation H for you.' When you go to your local, small-town *poitigéir*, you know they have a potion inside that'll fix you.

24 SAMHAIN / 24 NOVEMBER

Grianghraf
Photograph

[green-graf]

Tá m'fhón póca lán de ghrianghraif.
My mobile phone is full of photos.

I'd safely say I've about 7,500 photos on my mobile phone, as well as videos, a vast collection from home and my travels abroad. I always say I'll transfer them over to my computer, but I never do. I'll find photos from way back of my boys' first school days, national school Christmas concerts, Holy Communions and Confirmations, under-8 football blitzes and junior discos. Then there's graduation suit photos, bored young lads on Spanish sun holidays and happy faces at Croke Park. It's mad to think how the phone has consumed all our memories. It's an archive of our lives.

We have loads of photo albums in the house, but they are hidden away in presses and drawers, almost forgotten. I like putting photos in frames, so a few years ago I decided to dedicate one big wall in the house to family photos of all shapes and sizes. It came out great. Sometimes I stand there and smile about those moments, especially family portraits or the end-of-year national school photos where they would try to make my two boys look cute by getting them to lie down on the ground and put their chins in their hands. They'd run home from school with the photos and a price list to get them made into keyrings and T-shirts. It was a racket, but I'm glad I bought the photos, because having those pictures of them in their elastic ties on my family *grianghraf* wall is priceless.

25 SAMHAIN / 25 NOVEMBER

Crann troim
Elder tree

[crown trim]

D'úsáid na seandaoine an crann troim le haghaidh leigheasanna fadó.
The old folk used the elder tree for medicine long ago.

Elder, the Seeker
25 NOVEMBER–23 DECEMBER

If you were born between now and the last week of December, your Celtic tree is the elder, and you supposedly like a bit of adventure. I couldn't really find the exact translation for the elder tree in Irish, but *trom* is the Irish for 'elder' and 'elderberry' is *caor throim*, so it stands to reason that it's *crann troim*. The elderflower in spring will turn to elderberries in autumn, so you can buy yourself some elderberry syrup, or even collect the tiny dark purple berries to make your own.

26 SAMHAIN / 26 NOVEMBER

Ag spaisteoireacht
strolling through the countryside

[egg spash-tor-okht]

Bhí an chlann ag spaisteoireacht cois na habhann.
The family were strolling along by the river.

This word is for strolling through a forest or along the banks of a river. To me it always means following a lazy trail of a Sunday afternoon; there's no rush, no panic, the birds are chirping and the sky is blue. You park the car in Glendalough or Dún na Rí Forest Park to take the kids and the dog for a stroll. The kids are playing as they go along and the dog is happy because he's out pooing and sniffing everywhere. You could say you went for a walk, but that could mean a big hill walk; *ag spaisteoireacht* is leaving the house with no supplies, ambling along, not a care in the world.

I first used this word in Irish essays in school. Our teacher, Ms Walsh, would get us to write an essay every weekend, and every Monday morning you can be sure mine said I was out *ag spaisteoireacht*. You would use it in conversation rarely; it's a word for creative writing, in first and second year in secondary school, when you're trying to impress your teacher.

27 SAMHAIN / 27 NOVEMBER

Fuil
Blood

[fwill]

Doirtfear fuil ann.
There will be blood.

Blood is our lifeforce. You always have the impulse, when you cut your hand, to suck the wound straight away to clean it. And where there's fuil, *there are plasters.*

Smólach
Thrush

[smo-lokh]

D'eitil an smólach síos ar an ngéag.
The thrush flew down onto the branch.

29 SAMHAIN / 29 NOVEMBER

Cuimhne
Memory

[kwee-na (in Connemara), kwiv-na (in Munster)]

Tá cuimhní againn ar fad ar go leor rudaí.
We all have memories of many things.

I remember my nana showing me how to drink tea. I remember big velvet curtains in the sitting room. I remember my Hitachi vinyl record player. I remember the craic at lunchtimes behind the bicycle sheds in St Pat's Classical School. I remember getting teeth pulled to fit my braces. I remember someone drunk at midnight mass going up onto the sacred altar shouting and laughing. I remember Big Country in the RDS in 1983. I remember being 16 doing my Leaving Cert. I remember the *Rose of Aran* taking me out to Inis Meáin. I remember moving to the Basque Country. I remember getting my first job on TV with TG4. I remember the Soldiers of the Dawn on my breakfast radio show. I remember seeing my wife for the first time playing tunes in Donegal. I remember the days my sons came into this world. I remember the undertaker Paddy Fitzsimons stopping the traffic at the lights in town as my mother's funeral cortège came down the main street ... *Cuimhnígí i gcónaí ar bhur gcuimhní* (always remember your memories).

30 SAMHAIN / 30 NOVEMBER

Cnámh
Bone

[keh-nawv]

D'úsáid mé cnámha an turcaí le haghaidh stoic.
I used the turkey bones for stock.

The combination of the 'c' and 'n' so close together when I say this word almost makes me hear a bone snapping! There are more little fingers being broken on pitches all over the country than ever before. Whether it's the bones in your body, the bones in the fish you have to watch out for or the bones from the leg of chicken when you've eaten a snack box, it's cnámha.

1 NOLLAIG / 1 DECEMBER

Brat sneachta; calóg shneachta

Blanket of snow; snowflake

[brot shnokh-ta; cal-owg shnokh-ta]

Thosaigh na calóga sneachta ag titim taobh amuigh den fhuinneog.
The snowflakes started to fall outside the window.

Here's a double-header for you: the Irish for 'blanket of snow' and 'snowflake'. We see the first one only on occasion in Ireland, but I saw the mother of all blankets of snow in Siberia. I walked out of the airport in Tomsk and there were 25-foot snowdrifts, as high as the terminal. My leg would disappear a foot deep into the snow with every step, but it was soft snow that made that lovely 'crunch' sound as you walked on it. It never got slushy, like it does here.

We're always in awe of snow in Ireland, no matter what age we are – even if it's only a few flakes falling from the sky. You can use *calóg* from *calóg shneachta* in other places too, because it's the Irish for 'flake'. So you'd have *calóga arbhair* (cornflakes) for breakfast or have a Cadbury *Calóg* with your cup of tea – the crumbliest, flakiest *seacláid*. And if you have a friend who texts you ten minutes before you're supposed to meet to say they aren't coming, you can say, 'You're an awful *calóg*.'

If you learned Irish in school, you probably know *sneachta*, but take a minute to say it out loud and see how lovely it is to pronounce. A lot of us have these Irish words from school stored in the back of our minds somewhere, and we shouldn't be embarrassed to use them. You don't need to use full sentences. Just sprinkle little *calóga* of Irish into your conversations here and there, and it'll make your language richer.

2 NOLLAIG / 2 DECEMBER

Searbhasach
Sarcastic

[sha-roo-sokh]

Is maith liom nuair bhíonn duine searbhasach uaireanta.
I like when a person is sarcastic sometimes.

I feel like being sarcastic is part of who we are in Ireland. We're very good at it. I think we'd definitely be in the top ten sarcastic countries in the world. It's an art form.

Back in the day, me and the lads had a thing called 'the Navan sneer face'. Right around first year in secondary school when we were hanging out with all our friends, the level of sarcasm exploded, and we brought that sarcasm to the shopping centre in the form of the sneer face. We'd go there and say, 'Look at that over there', and put on our stupid sneer face and laugh at people. It's where we honed our humour.

There was a window between the ages of 10 and 12 when my youngest boy would do the Navan sneer face on command, but now that he's older and has inhibitions, it's gone. I could see the level of sarcasm in my boys rise when the junior discos were done, and now that they're young men, they have their own sneer faces. I'm in the Era of Sarcasm with my boys now. I'll get home from the other side of the world after travelling about 52,000 kilometres over two-and-a-half days, and they'll say, 'Look who's back from his holidays.' But *searbhas* is a form of slagging, and slagging means we love each other.

3 NOLLAIG / 3 DECEMBER

Córas
System

[chorus]

Tá an córas ag obair i gceart.
The system is working perfectly.

A boring word, but a good word. Here's a shout-out to the most famous córas *in Ireland:* CIÉ *or* Córas Iompair Éireann, *which roughly translates as the 'system to carry something from one place to another in Ireland'. I don't think it's doing a very good job.*

Fochupán
Saucer

[fuh-cup-awn]

Is breá le mo sheanmháthair fochupán lena cupán tae.
My granny loves a saucer with her cup of tea.

5 NOLLAIG / 5 DECEMBER

Deoir
Tear

[jore]

Bhí deoir i mo shúil agus mé ag éisteacht leis an amhrán.
There was a tear in my eye listening to the song.

As I'm writing this, I've just finished watching about 70 hours of the TV show *Yellowstone*. I've been on a journey with Kevin Costner, or should I say John Dutton. I know the ranch like the back of my hand – I know the road in and out, what the lodge looks like, where the sheds are, the names of all the horses. I feel as if I'm part of the Dutton family at this stage. I've even been on the Montana version of Daft looking for ranches. Most men love *Yellowstone* because they want to be cowboys, and I want to say publicly that there's not a straight man who's watched it who hasn't fallen in love with Beth Dutton. If my wife would let me put posters of Beth Dutton on my wall, I would.

I have lived and breathed and fantasised my way through the five seasons of the show over about a year and a half, and by the time I got to the end, I would fight to the death for the Duttons. I'd mobilise lads here in Claregalway if they needed any more cowboys to protect the ranch. And as I watched the final episode at two o'clock in the afternoon, sitting on the couch with no one around, I'm not afraid to admit that I shed a *deoir*.

6 NOLLAIG / 6 DECEMBER

Bronntanas
Present

[brun-tan-ass]

Cheannaigh mé bronntanas Nollag inniu.
I bought a Christmas present today.

You probably didn't realise you remembered this word until you saw it. It's another one like *sneachta* (snow, p. 320) that you probably already know if you learned Irish in school. *Bronntanas* slips nicely into English, if you're looking for an Irish word you can throw into conversation. It's a great one for the aunties and uncles arriving at the house a week before Christmas and saying to their nephew or niece, 'Here, I got you a little *bronntanas*. Put that under the tree.'

The word always brings me back to the Scalextric set me and my brothers got from Santa for Christmas. The anticipation of opening the box and putting the figure-of-eight track together, with the grandstands with the little people in them and the chequered flags! Now I get Happy Socks. I'd say I get three pairs every year for Christmas, but I can never find a matching set. I have shopping trolleys mixed with candy sticks and pool tables mixed with Winnebagos. They're lovely quality, but I can't take any more. I want you all to know that men don't want socks or Lynx sets or shower gel for their Christmas *bronntanais*; they want things like binoculars and Swiss Army knives.

7 NOLLAIG / 7 DECEMBER

Sciorr
Skid

[shkyur]

Sciorr an carr ar an leac oighir ar maidin.
The car skidded on the ice in the morning.

There was an area at the top of my road in Navan where a little turlough would form, and if it was wet just before a cold snap, it would turn into an ice rink. Me and my friends would all go there to slide around and mess. There was a hill beside it called Moate Hill, and when it snowed we would get old bags of fertiliser or sheets of corrugated iron and toboggan down. It was winter sports, Navan style.

One year it froze completely, and we were trying to be cool by skidding along the ice. We were getting better and better, showing off and throwing in little pirouettes, so I decided to try to skid across on my knees as if I'd just scored a goal. What I didn't realise was that there was a broken bottle under the snow, and I went across it on my knees at full speed. There was little pain and no blood, but I slit my kneecap. I had to get a few stitches and I still have a scar, but that put an end to my knee-*sciorr* days.

8 NOLLAIG / 8 DECEMBER

Flaithiúil
Generous

[flah-hool]

Bhí mo sheanathair flaithiúil.
My grandfather was generous.

My mother would have always said *flaithiúileach*. You might know this one, because it's one of those Irish words that's crept into our conversations. If your mam or dad or someone you know uses it, it's probably in relation to someone paying for things. It makes me think of the rich uncle who comes back from America and buys everyone a round in the pub, or the couple who have an open bar at their wedding. I also like *flúirseach*, which means 'abundant', like when the garden is in abundance in high summer – it even sounds like the English word 'flourishing'. We should all make an effort to be more *flaithiúil* – with praise and kindness and caring for others. If you're flourishing in all of those characteristics, it'll mean more for you and the people around you.

9 NOLLAIG / 9 DECEMBER

Spraoi
Craic, fun, divilment

[spree]

Bhí an-spraoi againn ag Electric Picnic.
We had great craic at Electric Picnic.

Spraoi *is divilment and craic, the highest level of fun you can have with your best mates. There's nothing more beautiful than when an Irish-speaking child from Connemara says, 'Spraoim peil' (I play football). It's colloquial to Connemara. We know* imrím *(I play), but* spraoim *is pure and beautiful, because it's playing for the craic.*

10 NOLLAIG / 10 DECEMBER

Cithfholcadh
Shower

[kih-hul-ka]

Bhí cithfholcadh fuar agam ar mhaidin.
I had a cold shower this morning.

My shower history has evolved tremendously over the years. In the 1960s-style basic bungalow I grew up in in Navan, we didn't have a shower – we had two rubber tubes like hosepipes that fitted onto the bath taps. I remember, on a Saturday night, me and my brothers having to take turns kneeling at the side of the bath with the Head & Shoulders because the ads made us all think we had dandruff at the age of 18 or 19. There was only so much hot water with the immersion being on, and if you were last to the rubber tubes, you'd have to finish off your hair with cold water.

During my student and Dublin years, the good aul Triton T-90 did the job. They had the noisy white shower box that clicked the extractor fan on – that's if you had an extractor fan in your rental accommodation. You knew when the shower was on back in those days, because the whole place would shake.

Years later, the fancy showerheads came into play. There were three settings on the one Dympna and I had in the en suite in our first house: drizzle, rain and full on. I think one of them might have been called the 'massage' setting. How happy we were to have an en suite! Now it's all about the rainfall showerhead – the big one overhead that really feels like being in the rain. Having said that, I have no doubt the Triton T-90 *cithfholcadh* is still going strong in households across Ireland.

11 NOLLAIG / 11 DECEMBER

Podchraoladh
Podcast

[pod-kray-la]

Ar chuala tú an podchraoladh nua ó Tommy, Hector agus Laurita?
Have you heard the new Tommy, Hector & Laurita podcast?

I sat down with Tommy to have a Covid coffee on Merchants Road in Galway in May 2020, when the world was upside down. We sat on an empty street, chatting away and hatching plans about the future – specifically, work in a lockdown future. First we talked about a new radio show, but that quickly changed to a *podchraoladh*. We called Laurita Blewitt in Mayo to tell her our idea and she was up for it. Mayo people are always up for it.

I borrowed a few podcast mics from Tree Bark Coffee in Moycullen, we had GarageBand on the laptop, and off we went to the shed down the bottom of Tommy's garden. It was called the Hen House. When we walked in, I pulled the curtains closed because I didn't want any distractions and I plugged everything in. We hadn't a clue what we were doing.

I'll never forget what Tommy said: 'Look, let's just keep talking and see what happens.' I'm smiling here thinking about that, because *so* much happened ...

12 NOLLAIG / 12 DECEMBER

Coinneal
Candle

[kwin-ill]

D'imigh an leictreachas aréir agus las mé na coinnle.
The electricity went last night and I lit the candles.

13 NOLLAIG / 13 DECEMBER

Sos
Break, rest

[suss]

Tógaimis sos.
Let's take a break.

This might be the simplest word of the whole year, a small word that has a lot of feeling when you use it. You can use it for a break at national school for lunch (*sos lóin*), a break for tea at work (*sos tae*), or a little weekend break away for a few days in Galway (*sos beag i nGaillimh*). A *sos* in Irish is like a siesta in Spain. We use siesta in English all the time without even blinking. But when we talk about having a snooze or a rest in the middle of the day, we should be saying *sos beag* – a small break. It's right there for us in our native language.

Everyone needs a *sos* in the middle of the day, whether it's a 'five minutes on the couch' *sos* or a 'sitting out the back garden with a cup of tea in the sunshine' *sos*. Let's get the word into our minds and let's everyone take a lovely *sos beag*.

14 NOLLAIG / 14 DECEMBER

I mbun (an tí)
In charge (of the house)

[ih mun (on tee)]

Cé atá i mbun an tí?
Who's in charge of the house?

When Mam and Dad leave for a weekend away, leaving the kids in charge of the house for the first time ever, their friends are over in jig time. Then you come back to half-drunk cans of Monster down the back of the couch and sticky kitchen floors from all the Smirnoff Ices. All dead giveaways that the teenagers have been i mbun an tí.

15 NOLLAIG / 15 DECEMBER

Dán

Poem

[dawn]

Chum me dán bheag le haghaidh an gheimhridh.
I wrote a small poem for the winter.

In honour of Christmas and the book, I've written you a little poem *as Gaeilge*. It sounds absolutely cat in English, but say it in Irish and get the rhyming going …

Tháinig an sneachta i lár na míosa,
Brait bhána ar fud na ngairdíní,
Le sioc agus fuacht, goimh agus gaoth,
Bhí an teas ar siúl ar fud an tí.

The snow came in the middle of the month,
White blankets all over the gardens,
With ice and cold, nippiness and wind,
The heating was on all over the house.

16 NOLLAIG / 16 DECEMBER

Geall
Promise

[gyall]

Geallaim duit nach ndéanfaidh mé arís é.
I promise you I'll never do it again.

When your mother is giving out to you and you say 'I swear I didn't', or when you make the sign of the cross on your neck and say, 'I promise I'll do that for you', you're making a gealltanas. Geall also means a bet, like a promise to the bookie to give them your money: Chuir mé geall ar an Grand National (I made a bet on the Grand National).

17 NOLLAIG / 17 DECEMBER

Maróg Nollag
Christmas pudding

[mar-owg null-eg]

Thosaigh m'aintín ag déanamh maróg na Nollag i mí Iúil.
My aunty started making the Christmas pudding in July.

I had a mighty set of aunties and they were all great pudding people. Country aunties are all great at the pavlova, apple tart and putting on a spread. Sandwiches always tasted better in your auntie's house. Every October, they were like a battalion, making a fleet of puddings that would be wrapped up in the *Meath Chronicle* and put deep in the hot press. Then the puddings would be unleashed on Christmas Day, the *pièce de résistance*. There was so much brandy in it, you'd nearly be intoxicated by the smell.

But you can't go straight from Christmas dinner to the pudding. You have to lie down first and watch a bit of *Wallace & Gromit* or *Top of the Pops* from 1983. Then you can come back for round two at ten o'clock at night, slice yourself a bit of pudding and have it with some warm custard. We don't make pudding in our house at Christmas, because I'm the only one who likes it – but my missus always buys me a tiny little Heston Blumenthal one from Marks & Spencer, because she knows I love my *maróg Nollag*.

18 NOLLAIG / 18 DECEMBER

Bosca bruscair
Rubbish bin

[buska broo-sker]

Bhí an bosca bruscair lán go béal.
The rubbish bin was full to the brim.

19 NOLLAIG / 19 DECEMBER

Glasra
Vegetable

[gloss-ra]

Bíonn glasraí difriúla i séasúr tríd an mbliain.
Different vegetables are in season throughout the year.

I want to give a shout-out to the greatest Christmas vegetable of all time: Brussels sprouts. I buy my sprouts every December from Terryland Fruit & Veg Market. You can buy every fruit on the planet in Terryland, and it's in the middle of Galway. I get big vines of Brussels sprouts, and it's amazing to see them all attached to the strong stalk. It's a real Christmas moment for me.

Brussels sprouts are brilliant because loads of them are grown locally, especially in and around north County Dublin and Meath. There are some farmers who only grow sprouts, and I salute the people who produce these unbelievable vegetables, because what would Christmas dinner be without a mound of Brussels sprouts? Hundreds of thousands of them are grown every year to be put on plates all across the country on this one day. They're brilliant little Irish *glasra* balls.

20 NOLLAIG / 20 DECEMBER

Síob; Síob abhaile
Lift; Lift home

[shee-uhb; shee-uhb ah-wall-ya]

An bhfuil síob uait abhaile go Ciarraí?
Do you need a lift home to Kerry?

You come home from Sydney for Christmas and you go down to the local pub. You're meeting everyone and you have a few pints of stout and the craic is great. Then it's last orders and they close, and there's no local taxi, because you live in the middle of nowhere ... and your friend who's been sipping 7UP all night offers you a lift home. The lift home is as much a part of the enjoyment of the night as the pints.

There's nothing better if you're working in Microsoft in Dublin and you're in the canteen, and Joe who's from just down the way in Tralee says to you, 'What day are you finishing up on, the 22nd? Do you want a lift to Kerry?' A lift to Kerry, for fuck's sake! Imagine the joy at being offered that. You just have to throw all your bags in the boot and you're getting a lift to your door. And as soon as your feet cross the threshold, you're back out again to your local to meet your mates, and hopefully there's a *síob abhaile* for you there too.

I've got a lift home from the pub at Christmas a few times and it's just a beautiful thing, because that designated driver has given you a gift. Everyone is in high spirits, you leave the warm pub to go out into the frosty night and hop in the car, and they drop you to your gate. Irish people cherish a *síob abhaile*.

21 NOLLAIG / 21 DECEMBER
Grianstad an Gheimhridh / Winter Solstice

Chuile
Every

[hwil-ah]

Chuile Nollaig téimid abhaile go Gaillimh.
Every Christmas we go home to Galway.

Every December when we were kids, my mam would say, 'We're going to Tuam for Christmas.' It was her home, and it felt like home to us. These were the days when my dad had Wolverine-style sideburns and wore a pinstripe suit, like all Irish dads in the 1970s. He drove the same car as most other dads, too – either a Ford Cortina or an Opel Grenada. Our car of choice was a red Cortina, reg 3803ZU, and we would pile into it, ready to start the five-hour journey from Navan to Galway.

I remember the route like the back of my hand. We'd go from Navan to Athboy to Delvin to Horseleap. In Horseleap, we would turn right over a little bridge and head to Moate and on to Athlone. Then, as we came into Ballyforan, me and my brothers would be elbowing each other and laughing because we would cross the River Suck.

'Dad, Dad! What's the name of the river?'

'That's the Suck out there, boys. Look at the Suck.'

Then we would stop at the same tree on the Bog Road near Mountbellew every year, where Dad would carve all our names into the bark with a penknife. We would hit the road again, turn right at the agricultural college and drive to Barnaderg – which always fascinated me, because even though it's called 'Red Gap', no one ever seemed to use its English name. Outside Barnaderg there was a tiny crooked bridge, and that's where the chorus of 'Are we there yet?' would start from us in the back seat. Finally, we would arrive in Tuam and we'd know that we were home in Galway for Christmas. The exact same trip with the exact same stops, *chuile Nollaig*.

22 NOLLAIG / 22 DECEMBER

Margadh
Market

[mar-a-ga]

Bíonn margadh Nollag ar siúl gach bliain.
There's a Christmas market on every year.

I was on the dole for a year or two when I moved back from the Basque Country, so one day around November time I came up with an idea to sell some Christmas decorations at the local market. The Galway market has been going for years; it's an institution in the city. It has the feel of a proper market: stalls selling Celtic jewellery and incense holders, funky art by local artists, candles, amazing cheese, fruit and veg, mobile juice bars, street food, hippies with their dogs – bohemian vibes and eclectic colour everywhere. It's a small market, but even on the coldest of winter Saturdays, it's always warm and buzzy.

My plan was to make ornate, earthy Christmas centrepieces for tables: a nice pot full of scented pine cones. I collected hundreds of cones in the grounds of NUIG, doused them in orange, clove and cinnamon tinctures and sealed them in bags for weeks. I bought a hundred pots from the garden centre, a hundred chunky red and silver candles, and lovely tartan and red ribbons so I could finish off the pots with bows. I'll never forget opening the sealed bags after four weeks soaking in the oils – perfect! My mam came down to help me and Dympna make up the pots the day before the market. It was frosty and dry, a few days before Christmas, and I got a table in a nice position really early. I sold the lot – 25 quid a pop and €2,500 cash in my pocket. That's what you call *lá maith ag an margadh* – a good day at the market.

23 NOLLAIG / 23 DECEMBER

Clampar
Racket, furore

[klomper]

Bhí clampar ceart ag teacht ón gcóisir tí aréir.
There was a right racket coming from the house party last night.

This is a word for when the party is in full revelry, when every single person you know is in the pub or at the house party. It's a right rowdy shindig, the kind when you have to go outside to take a phone call and you can still hear the clampar.

24 NOLLAIG / 24 DECEMBER

Crann beithe
Birch tree

[krawn beh-ha]

Bhí am ann fadó nuair a bhíodh crainn bheithe ag fás gach áit sa tír.
There was a time, long ago, when birch trees grew everywhere in the country.

Birch, the Achiever
24 DECEMBER–20 JANUARY

If you were born at this time of year, your Celtic tree is the birch. Birch people are resilient. They'll always stand up and stand out in the crowd. You'll recognise birches from their white, ash-coloured bark. When I look out my kitchen window, I see a line of *crainn bheithe*. It's one of the first trees I planted in my garden. I see them through the seasons of the year, and they've become my friends. They're resilient in the winter time and thrive through the summer.

25 NOLLAIG / 25 DECEMBER
Lá **Nollag** / Christmas Day

Ar maos
Soaking

[air mwee-as]

Ná déan dearmad an liamhás a chur ar maos roimh an Nollaig.
Don't forget to soak the ham before Christmas.

I think we all carry things that our mothers and fathers did in the kitchen when we were younger with us into our own kitchens as we get older. Their tricks of the trade, little things you do to prepare the food for special occasions. There's something special about the dinner on Christmas Day; it has to be the most eagerly anticipated dinner of the year. It's the mixture of all the stuff: the flavour, the *glasraí* (vegetables, p. 338), the roast potatoes, the stuffing, the gravy, the turkey and, of course, the ham. I. LOVE. HAM.

The night before the big day, huge lumps of ham are soaked in the biggest saucepans people can get their hands on in houses all over the country. It's the start of the culinary journey. Then it's ready for cooking on Christmas Day. We've become passionate about making glazes in our house in the last few years; we all love it. You can enjoy a bit of ham with the dinner, but is there anything better than going to the kitchen hours later, after the Trivial Pursuit, the Bond movies and the big clean-up, to feast on it again? You stand in the kitchen at midnight just eating morsels of ham. And the *cur ar maos* makes all the difference.

26 NOLLAIG / 26 DECEMBER
Lá Fhéile Stiofáin / St Stephen's Day

Sladmhargadh
Bargain

[slad-wawr-ih-ga]

Bíonn go leor sladmhargaí sna siopaí théis Nollag.
There are loads of bargains in the shops after the Christmas.

The RTÉ News religiously does a story about the queues on St Stephen's Day every year: 'There were big crowds outside Brown Thomas this morning at 7 a.m. as the sales opened.' This is a word for the people who get a kick out of sales, the real sealgairí sladmhargadh (*bargain hunters*).

27 NOLLAIG / 27 DECEMBER

Traochta
Exhausted

[tray-okh-ta]

Bhíomar ar fad traochta théis an turais fhada abhaile ón aerfort. We were all exhausted after the long journey home from the airport.

Your sister, your brother-in-law who you don't get on with and their four kids have just left the house to go back to Cork after staying with you for the last two days. The house is in bits, you don't know what day of the week it is and you're fed up eating turkey. *Traochta* is a great word for describing how you feel after you've had 17 people over for Christmas dinner and nine of them stayed the night, so there are makeshift beds in every room and there's not a clean towel left in the house. Finally, you can sit down on the couch with nobody nagging the head off you and watch whatever TV programmes you like.

There's no nationality in the world better at describing being tired than Irish people, because we're never just tired, we're exhausted. And don't be afraid to use *tuirseach traochta* to say you're *really* exhausted – it's probably how you're feeling on this very day, 27 December, when everyone has finally left. So make yourself a nice glazed ham sandwich and put your feet up. You must be wrecked.

28 NOLLAIG / 28 DECEMBER

Réinfhia
Reindeer

[rain-ee-ah]

Chonaic mé réinfhia den chéad uair thuas san Iorua.
I saw a reindeer for the first time in Norway.

29 NOLLAIG / 29 DECEMBER

Clapsholas
Dusk

[klop-hull-ass]

Bhí an tuath ciúin agus an clapsholas ag titim.
The countryside was quiet as dusk fell.

Dusk conjures up an image of sitting at a lake and you see three or four birds flying across the sky. You always want to be outside when you're describing clapsholas. *It's the closing of light, the gateway to night-time.*

30 NOLLAIG / 30 DECEMBER

Líofa
Fluent

[lee-uff-a]

Ba bhreá liom a bheith líofa sa teanga.
I'd love to be fluent in the language.

This is the second-last word in the book on purpose; I suppose it's a bit of a message. You've been on a journey through the year with me in Irish, so I feel it's important to remind you that I wasn't born into the Irish language. I didn't grow up in the Gaeltacht or an Irish-speaking household. The doors of the language opened up to me and I walked in.

Being *líofa* is what we all want when learning a new language; it's a beautiful thing when you can say, '*Tá mé beagnach líofa sa Ghaeilge*' (I'm almost fluent in Irish). But this is a word for ye, *na Gaeilgeoirí* of all levels *amuigh ansin* (out there). There are many steps on the way to being *líofa*, and just because you're not there yet doesn't mean the Irish language isn't yours to use. A word here and there will turn into a sentence here and there; then you can have conversations *as Gaeilge*. Because when you love the language, it's easier to learn it.

I've opened up the doors of the Irish language to you in this book. Now it's up to you to walk on through. *An dtiocfaidh tú isteach?*

31 NOLLAIG / 31 DECEMBER

An todhchaí
The future

[on tow-khee]

Ag deireadh na bliana, smaoinímid i gcónaí ar an todhchaí.
At the end of the year, we always think about the future.

It's New Year's Eve, *Oíche Chinn Bliana*, and tomorrow is the future. So I want to give a New Year's blessing to all the disciples of Irish: the hardcore heads, the word wizards, the language lovers and the Irish-curious.

We had a driver when we were filming in Antigua and his name was Chalice. He was a Rastafari in a HiAce, and every time I got back to the van, the two of us would have the same call and response:

'Blessings!' he'd say.

'Every time,' I'd say.

Now I'm passing that blessing on to you for *an todhchaí*, but I'm giving it to you in Irish. So when we meet each other in the petrol station or the supermarket or the airport, don't forget to say '*Beannachtaí!*' and I'll say, '*An t-am ar fad.*'

Go Raibh Míle Maith Agaibh

An Ghaeilge

Tá Sí Ag Teacht!